VICTORY IN FAILURE

VICTORY IN FAILURE

ALEXANDER MACLAREN

Selected and edited by WILLIAM J. PETERSEN

Introduction by WARREN WIERSBE

Illustrations by RON McCARTY

KEATS PUBLISHING, INC.   NEW CANAAN, CONNECTICUT

The material in this book has been selected and edited from *The Christian World Pulpit Magazine, The Expository Times, The Life of David, The Christian Commonwealth Magazine*

VICTORY IN FAILURE

Shepherd Illustrated Classic Edition published in 1980

Selection and special contents of this edition copyright © 1980 by Keats Publishing, Inc.

All Rights Reserved

Library of Congress Catalog Number: 79-88309

ISBN:0-87983-212-6

Printed in the United States of America

SHEPHERD ILLUSTRATED CLASSICS are published by Keats Publishing, Inc. 36 Grove Street, New Canaan, Connecticut 06840

CONTENTS

INTRODUCTION BY WARREN WIERSBE

VICTORY IN FAILURE	3
NEW NAMES FOR OVERCOMERS	15
ON THE WINNING SIDE	27
LIVING IN THE LIGHT OF VICTORY	37
VICTORY OVER THE LAST ENEMY	49
THE VICTORIOUS TOUCH	63
WHAT IT TAKES TO WIN	77
THIRST FOR GOD	89
YOUR INHERITANCE IS WAITING	103
VICTORY OVER COLDNESS	115
FOOTSTEPS TO FORGIVENESS	125
VICTORY OVER DARKNESS	145
FAITH IS THE VICTORY	159
THE GOOD NEWS OF GLORY	173

Illustrations

Jesus talking to disciples, seated in the upper room
Jesus healing Peter's mother-in law of her fever
Jesus holds a Roman coin
The prophet Nathan confronts King David
Man kneeling before Jesus

INTRODUCTION TO THE SHEPHERD CLASSICS EDITION

The Victorian Age boasted a galaxy of great preachers, perhaps unparalleled in history; and among the greatest of them was Dr. Alexander Maclaren. As you read this book, you will understand why.

I think it was Dr. Peter Marshall who said that, if a man wanted to become a great preacher, he must first arrange to be born in Scotland. Maclaren qualified: he was born February 11, 1826, in Glasgow. In reviewing his life, I was amazed to discover that Maclaren lived through the entire Victorian Age. He was eleven years old when Victoria was crowned, and the queen had been dead nine years when Maclaren passed away on May 5, 1910, in Edinburgh. The Erie Canal was a year old when Maclaren was born, and seven years before he died, the Wright brothers opened the "air age" at Kitty Hawk.

Maclaren was converted as a child and was baptized on May 17, 1840. One day his father took him to Rev. Charles Stovel to see if the pastor thought the lad fit for the ministry. Stovel's reply has turned out to be a masterpiece of understatement: "Well, well, perhaps he might." The examiner at the Baptist College in Stepney had keener discernment for when Maclaren applied at the age of sixteen, the examiner said to his own son: "We have accepted today a young Scotsman *who will cut you all out!*"

The young Scotsman lived up to that prophecy and excelled in his studies, particularly Bible languages. Unfortunately, many preachers either neglect or forsake their Hebrew and Greek after they graduate but not Maclaren. It was his practice to spend two hours each day reading his Bible in the original languages. He did not parade his scholarship in the pulpit, but the results of that scholarship, when mixed with his own deep piety, produced some of the greatest expositions of Scripture found anywhere in the English language.

On November 16, 1845, Maclaren was sent to preach at a run-down chapel in Southampton. The people at Portland Chapel were so impressed that they asked him to preach for three months as a "trial ministry." Maclaren ended by being their pastor for twelve years. During those years he saw the work take on new life, gain an enviable reputation in the area, and become known as a center for the preaching of the Word.

When he celebrated his fiftieth year in the ministry in 1896, Maclaren told a gathering of friends: "I thank God that I was stuck down in a quiet little obscure place to begin my ministry. . . . I thank God for the early days of struggle and obscurity."

That obscurity ended when he was called to pastor the large and influential Union Chapel, Oxford Road, Manchester. The church was interdenominational in make-up, requiring only that the minister be a Baptist and that believers' baptism by immersion be the only mode practiced. He began his ministry in Manchester in July, 1858, and closed it the last Sunday in June, 1903.

Whatever else the congregation may have expected of their new pastor, he let it be known that he would focus his attention on studying and preaching the Word of God. "The secret of success for a minister," he once said, "is that he should concentrate his intellectual force on the one work of preaching." Union Chapel housed a large congregation, but before long the congregation

Introduction

was too large for the facilities and a new church building had to be built. It seated nearly 2000 people and was usually filled.

Maclaren was not one to use promotional schemes to get a crowd. His close friend, and editor, W. Robertson Nicoll, wrote: "But statistics, organization, machinery, crowds, elaborate music, display, advertising—these things were not to his taste." Special services were also not to his taste, and throughout his life he courageously said "No!" to invitations to preach at such occasions. His study, his home, and his pulpit were the centers around which his quiet but effective ministry revolved.

It is as an expositor of the Bible that Maclaren is remembered. "I have tried to make my ministry a ministry of exposition of Scripture," he told guests at his Ministerial Jubilee in 1896. "I have tried to preach Jesus Christ." During the years of his ministry, German "higher criticism" threatened the foundations of orthodox theology, liberalism invaded British politics, and great social problems challenged the government; yet you will find none of these matters dealt with in Maclaren's sermons. His philosophy was that of the old Puritan preacher who said, "Since so many are preaching to the times, you will not mind if I preach for eternity."

For this reason, Maclaren's sermons have a timeless quality about them. At a joint meeting of the Baptist and Congregational Unions in Joseph Parker's City Temple in London, Maclaren declared: "How unworthy it is for him [the preacher] to direct his telescope from the heaven of the Word to the low levels of current topics!" We who read his messages today are grateful that he held such a high view of preaching.

Maclaren had no plans for publishing any of his messages. However, a member of the church took down his sermons in shorthand during his first year in Manchester, and *Sermons Preached in Manchester* was the result. Ten years later, a second series was published. Those of us who have taught preachers have warned our students, "Don't read Maclaren during your sermon preparation—you will be tempted to preach his sermons!" Many preachers in Maclaren's day did plagiarize his material. While on a holiday in Devonshire, an officer of Union Chapel heard his pastor's sermons preached in an Anglican Church in the morning and a Weslyan Church in the evening!

As good as his published sermons are, it is Maclaren's *Exposition of Holy Scripture* that has given him a permanent and honored place in the ministerial hall of fame. It was his friend W. Robertson Nicoll, editor of *The Expositor* and *The British Weekly*, who first suggested the series to Maclaren when the preacher retired in 1903. Maclaren had outlines of his expository messages from the beginning of his ministry, so it was only a matter of expanding them and putting "flesh on the bones." The first volume on Genesis appeared in 1904, and other volumes were published regularly until the set reached a total of 32 volumes.

Because he was an expositor of the Word, Maclaren allowed the Scriptures to speak for themselves. He did not find sensational topics and then look for some Bible passage to support his own already-formed ideas. He came to the Bible and sought for the message that God had for him in a given passage. His outlines were not manufactured and superimposed upon Scripture. They came out of the Scriptures, and they permitted the Scriptures to reveal the timeless truths that must always be the themes of evangelical preaching. Often, after reading one of his masterful expositions, I have said to myself, "Now, why didn't *I* see that? It's right there!"

Introduction

Because of the success of his books, Maclaren died a wealthy man. An ex-president of the Baptist Union of Great Britain once complained: "Don't mention Alexander Maclaren to me! He died a very wealthy man and did not leave a penny to any Baptist charity or denominational cause!"

But Maclaren has left us a wealth of sermonic material that can enrich us for eternity. You will find your own spiritual life challenged and strengthened as you permit Alexander Maclaren to make the eternal Word of God real for your life today. Don't expect to meet the preacher, but the preacher's God and Savior. "To efface one's self is one of a preacher's first duties," he said. "The herald should be lost in his message."

And now—to the message!

Warren W. Wiersbe
Chicago, Illinois
June, 1980

VICTORY IN FAILURE

The writings of
Alexander Maclaren

VICTORY IN FAILURE

Be of good cheer; I have overcome the world.
(JOHN 16:33)

"Be of good cheer, I have overcome the world"

SO SAID CHRIST when within an hour of Gethsemane and a day of Calvary. It is a strange utterance for such a moment, and seemingly altogether contradicted by fact.

If this were victory, to have failed in the effort to win men to goodness, to have spoken words of gentleness and truth which next to nobody cared to hear, and to have given counsels which no man regarded, to have been misunderstood, rejected, hated, to have lived a life of poverty and loneliness, and to have died in the first flush of early manhood, unlamented save by a handful of bewildered apostles and two or three brave women, if this is victory what would be defeat. And yet this calm utterance of triumph is our Lord's summing up of His whole life.

Looking back he sees it as all one continuous victory. Looking forward He sees the cross as already overcome though yet to be endured, and in that apparently crushing defeat. He recognises crowning victory. If Jesus Christ was right, most men are wrong. If that life is the type of a victorious life many of us need to revise our notions and to revolutionize our practices.

Now these words suggest to me three questions.

What is a victorious life?

Was there ever such a life?

If there was, what does it matter to me?

And the answer to all three questions lies in this shout of victory from the Man who was within arm's length of His Cross: "Be of good cheer; I have overcome the world."

VICTORY IN FAILURE

So, then, let me ask you to think with me, what, in the light of this great saying, we must believe to be a victorious life—"I have overcome the world." People say in what they choose to call the Johannine writings there is a peculiar phraseology—which I take leave to think John learned from Jesus—and one of the characteristics of that phraseology is the meaning that is attached to that expression—"the world." I suppose you understand, that by that verse is not meant this great assemblage of wonder and beauty which God has spread around us and set us to live in and understand; but that it means two things—first, the whole mass and aggregate of visible and sensible things considered as apart from God; and next substantially what you and I mean when we talk about Society—an aggregate of godless men. These two things—the material universe apart from God, and the men who make a unity because they are apart from Him, these two thoughts cover ground which John and John's Master desired to include within this term.

Now, then, if that is the meaning of the phrase, let us take another step. What is it here for? Two things; first, for the same purpose as the leaping poles and bars and other things in a gymnasium are, to make muscle, to build character; by resistance to make us strong. And another thing, for the same purpose as the window is in the house, that through it we may look and see the sun. And just as a man may fix his eyes upon some beauty of colored glass in the window, and look at that oblivious of the more glorious, diviner coloring laid on by no human brush beyond, you and I, by our weakness make the world—which is meant by its visibilities to show us the invisible, even His eternal power and Godhead—an abstraction, instead of a transparent medium. And just as men may fail rightly to use the gymnastic apparatus, so

Victory in Failure

we by reason of our weakness find that the world robs us of our strength, instead of increasing our strength, seduces instead of stimulating us, and draws us away from our true selves and the home of our soul, which is God Himself.

And so, the world conquers us when we let it hinder us from living Christ-like and God-pleasing lives; the world conquers us when it fills our affection and constitutes our aim; the world conquers us when it lets down its painted phantasms between us and the true realities, the things unseen, and eternal, and universal.

We conquer the world when nothing in it will turn our feet one inch from the straight path, when all that is in it will exercise our muscles and build up our character, and when like some Jacob's ladder with its foot upon the earth we climb by its gradual rounds until we reach at last the summit and gaze into the face that is above it, the face of our God.

The one is to be beaten by the world; the other is to beat it. And when you put your foot on the animal that is in you, when you refuse to be deceived by the world's false promises or caught by its glittering baits, when you will not let its siren voices seduce you into ignoble contempt with its trivialities and transparencies, then you have conquered. Otherwise you are conquered.

Now all that is threadbare. Aye, and threadbare things need to be rung into men's ears over and over again, until the threadbare things have become the sovereign laws of their lives. And there never was a time, I suppose, when there was more need for our preaching what is the true type of a successful life, and what is the true meaning of a life that is a failure than there is to-day.

There is many a rich man whom the hosannas of the Stock Exchange declare to be wonderfully successful, who from the highest point of view, the only true point of view, is a dead failure. He has gained all that he desired. Yes, and has he conquered the world, or has the world conquered him? Has it helped him to see God? Has it helped him to be a man? Or has it hid God from him and turned him into a money-bag? Success? Yes. A victorious life? Yes.

Do you remember the old story about the soldier that shouted out that he had caught a prisoner. And the officer said, "Bring him along." And the soldier answered, "But he won't come." "Then come yourself." And the answer was, "He won't let me."

That is the kind of victory over the world that many of our successful people have got; these are so hampered and held in its chains that early noble visions have passed away, and are smiled at now, and God and His angels are a great deal further off from the successful man than they were from the striving youth. The true prize may have been won by some poor old woman in her garret, or by some man who is regarded as having been an utter failure in the race, and who, having missed all the other prizes, has got this one, a spirit being molded into the Christ likeness and an eye which ever looks beyond the things seen and temporal to Him who is Himself eternal.

If we will not let the world, either the aggregate of material things, or Society, with its maxims and ways, hinder us from the noble life; if we will not allow it to prevent us, but use it to aid us in seeing God, in loving Him, in doing our duty for His dear sake; then, however solitary and sad and unsuccessful my life may otherwise be, I have conquered; and all else is defeat. So that is the answer to my first question.

And now for my second question: Was there ever such

a life? Jesus Christ in our text says that His was. And here is an odd thing, that nobody is revolted by the apparent self-complacency of the speech, and that the world takes Jesus Christ at His own valuation, and says, "Yes, it is true; Thou hast overcome, and Thou only." Now, if we look at the words from that point of view, notice how profound an insight they give us into the whole life of Jesus Christ as it is mirrored in His memory and His conscience.

Do not let us be mealy-mouthed, or afraid of marring the great doctrine of His divinity, when we give the fullest meaning to that word overcome. It was no sham fight, no dramatic spectacle, an exhibition for the edification of those that here heard of it that he fought in the wilderness. True there was no nidus, nest, or occasion, for the temptation within; but, equally true, the temptation when it came to Him did present what was a temptation to His humanity, and here He resisted it and overcame. And you do not understand the wondrous beauty, the wondrous calm, the universal compassion, the undisturbed leisureliness, as it were, of that life if you do not see beneath all the gentleness, the tenderness, the care for others, the open eye to everything that was fair and good, the stern and continual stress of one good purpose that was resisted by things around, but was ever borne onwards by His submission.

I have seen in one of our Lancashire manufactories a machine by which a great solid block of India rubber is pressed by a strong spring continually against a sharp-cutting edge. That was like Jesus Christ; the humanity conscious of all the pain and sorrow, and the unmoved will which was the result of an unchanging love, and had for its consequence an infinite sacrifice; the unmoved will bore up ever against the cutting edge, the sensitive heart of the Man of Sorrows. It was a real conquest from the beginning to the end; none the less because through all the conflict there was calm, and at every round victory. That is the other thing that is here as mirrored in our Lord's consciousness in reference to His own individual life, an unbroken and continuous triumph. He never let one word pass from His lips to suggest even a momentary reverse in the conflict. Other men may press on in the main on the right lines, but the right line for the best of us is like the unsteady strokes that the child draws when it first gets a pen into his hands. Christ's life is unbending, one continous straight line, ever directed to the cross, and seen through the gloom of the cross, to the Throne that is beyond.

As I said a moment ago, when He says "I have overcome the world," nobody stands up and says, "It is a piece of insane presumption." Everybody, except some poor sceptical people who want to make a reputation by not saying what anybody else said, all the world bows down before Him and says, "Thou art beautiful, Thou are fair, one entire and perfect chrysolite without a flaw." Do you ever think how strange it is that we let Jesus Christ, if I may so put it, say things about Himself without in the least degree detracting from the Majesty of perfection that we carry in our minds, that we would never tolerate from anybody else?

"I am meek and lowly in heart." Think of a man saying that. Why if anybody else said it, the answer would be—and it would be a right answer—"Meek and lowly! If you were, you never would have said so." But when Jesus Christ says it, we accept it, and it does not, as I said, in the smallest degree detract from, rather it enhances the image of stainless unworldliness and superhuman beauty which we all recognise in Him. And so He looks back upon His life.

But the words of my text have not only a retrospective but an immediate prospective aspect, for we cannot but suppose that they are what critics call the prophetic perfect, "I have overcome." There was the cross tomorrow, it was to be endured yet; but it was behind Him in one aspect, for He had accepted it, and therefore He had overcome it.

Let us take the lesson: the way to overcome our troubles is to bear them; the way to conquer our crosses is willingly to lay them on our shoulders. The acceptance of them is a pointless arrow. He that will not allow the sharpest of the world's possible penalties to cause him to deflect one hair's-breadth from the path of duty, he has overcome the penalty and the pain, even before his flesh has to bear it.

But there is another thought here. I cannot discharge from these triumphant words, "I have overcome the world," a prophetic look into a more distant future than the Calvary of to-morrow; Christ's cross is the victory over the world. "Now is the judgment of this world; now shall the Prince of this world be cast out." There all men may see what sin is and what sin leads to; there all men may learn the hollowness of the world; there all men may behold the sacrifice for the world's sins; there all men may find new motives and new powers for their own conflict with their own world. And so, not only in reference to His own past life, not in reference only to His immediate death upon the cross, but in reference to the ultimate results of that Passion—results which the world's history ever since more and more has been showing, are being wrought out, and will be completely accomplished yet, Jesus Christ triumphantly declared, "I have overcome the world;" and answered for us all the question, Was ever such a life lived?

If such a life has been lived, what does it matter to me? My text answers in a very remarkable collocation of phrases—"Be ye of good cheer; I have overcome." That is what it matters to us; that is altogether unlike what it would be possible for any other body to say, or if he did he would lay himself open to a very damaging answer: "I have overcome the world! Well, so much the better for you; but what good is that to me? Your example may stimulate me; it may lift me up when my life is over, and do me good in a hundred different ways, but it is not enough, not half enough for my necessities."

Contrast with this saying of our Lord's a saying of His servant Paul's, which looks very like it, but is in reality infinitely different from it: "I have fought the good fight; I have finished my course; I have kept the faith." So he said to Timothy; but there is not a hint in Paul's mind that his completing the course and keeping the faith was of any good to Timothy, except as a bracing memory and a stimulating example. But Jesus to each of us says, "You cheer up, I have conquered."

Look again at my text, at its immediate context, and notice, just before, our Lord has said this: "In the world ye shall have tribulation; in Me ye shall have peace." Very well; there are two spheres, if I may so say, in both of which the Christian man dwells—in the world and in Christ—the one full of afflictions and trials and temptations; the other like some sequestered dale in the midst of an island in the raging sea, where the wind never blows, and all is peace. In Christ peace; in the world tribulation; and if we overcome the world it must be because Christ is more for us than an example, be-

Victory in Failure

cause through His death on the cross we have communion with Him; His Spirit of life flows into our spirit, and we in Him, as well as by Him, are conquerors.

The answer to this final question, What does it matter to me? is still further supplied by the words of the evangelist himself. Jesus has shown us how His victory is to be our triumph in the words I have quoted, and John, long, long after, when old age had removed the Master far enough away to see Him more clearly, supplemented and echoed the words of my text when he said, "This is the victory that overcometh the world, even our faith."

You put your trust in Him as the Sacrifice for your sins, and as the spirit of your lives you look to Him not only as example, not only as pattern, but as power; you think of Him, not only as dying on the cross for you, but as living in you, and then you will find, as sure as He lives, you will find that He has conquered, and that His conquest is for you. He, if I may so say it, has transfixed the dragon through its ugly head, and all the rest is but the lashings of its tail. He has bound the strong man; He has beaten the world and captured the central fortress, and the rest is an affair of outposts.

So be of good cheer; you will have to fight, thank God for it, you will have to fight; you will be beaten as sure as you live if you try to master the world without Jesus; but if you will lay your hands by faith on the head of that Lamb of God, and if you will open your hearts and your lives to the influences of His triumphant Spirit, then He will give you a share in His conflict, His conquest, and His royal repose, according to His own wonderful promise, "To him that overcometh will I grant to sit with Me on My throne, even as I overcame, and am set down with My Father on His throne."

NEW NAMES FOR OVERCOMERS

To him that overcometh will I give . . . a new name . . . which no man knoweth saving he that receiveth it.

(REV. 2:17)

ABRAHAM AND JACOB, in the Old Testament, received new names from God; Peter and the sons of Zebedee, in the New Testament, received new names from Christ. In the sad latter days of the Jewish monarchy, its kings, being deposed by barbarian and pagan conquerors, were reinstated, with new names imposed upon them, by the victors. In all these cases the imposition of the new name implies authority and ownership on the part of the giver; and generally a relationship to the giver, with new offices, functions, and powers on the part of the receiver.

And so when Christ from the heavens declares that He will rename the conqueror, He asserts, on the one hand, His own absolute authority over him, and, on the other hand, His own perfect knowledge of the nature and inmost being of the creature He names. And, still further, He gives a promise of a nature renewed, of new functions committed to the conqueror, of new spheres, new closeness of approach to Himself, new capacities, and new powers. Can we go any further?

Two things shine out plain and clear in the midst of the darkness and vagueness that surround the future glories of the redeemed. The one is their closer relationship to Jesus Christ; the other is their possession, in the ultimate and perfect state, of a body of which the predicates are incorruption, glory, power, and which is a fit organ for the spirit, even as the present corporeal house in which we dwell is an adequate organ for the animal life, and for that alone. And if we hold fast to these two things—the closer proximity to the Lord, and the wondrous new relations into which we may enter with the old Christ, and, on the other hand, the emancipation from the limitations imposed upon will and perception and action by the feeble body, and the possession of an instrument which is up to all the requirements of the immortal spirit and works in perfect correspondence with it—we can at least see such things as the following.

The "new name" means new vision. We know not how much the flesh, which is the organ of perception for things sensible, is an obscuring, blind, and impenetrable barrier between us and the loftier order of things unseen, in which this little sphere of the material and visible floats, perishable as a soap-bubble with its iridescent hues. But this we know, that when the stained glass of life is shattered, the white light of eternity will pour in. And this we know, "Now we see through a glass darkly: then, face to face." By reason of the encompassing flesh, we see but a reflection of the light. According to the great myth of the old Greek philosopher, which Paul, in the words quoted, has put his "Amen" to, we stand as in a cavern with our back to the light, and we see the shadows reflected passing before the mouth. But then, with the new name and the closer relationship to Jesus Christ, we shall turn ourselves from the reflections and to the light, and shall see face to face.

The "new name" means new activities. We know not how far these fleshly organs, which are the condition of our working upon the outward universe with which they bring us into connection, limit and hem the operations of the spirit. But this we know, that when that which is sown in weakness is raised in power, when that which is sown in corruption is raised in incorruption when that which is sown in dishonor is raised in glory, we shall then possess an instrument adequate to all that we can ask it to perform—a perfect tool for a perfected spirit. And, just as the fisherman, when he was taken from his nets to be an Apostle, was rechristened, so the saint, who has been working here, down amidst the trivialities of this poor material world, and learning his trade thereby, shall, when he is made a journeyman and set free from his apprenticeship, be renamed in token of larger functions on a nobler sphere and wider service with better implements. "His servants shall serve him." The strengths that have been slowly matured here, and the faculties which have been patiently polished and brought to an edge, shall find their true sphere in work, of sorts unknown, to which, perhaps, the conditions of space that now hamper us shall be no impediment.

Further, the "new name" means new purity. There are two words very characteristic of this Book of the Apocalypse. One of them is that word of my text, "new"—the "new Jerusalem," "new heavens," and a "new earth," a "new song," a "new name," and the grand, all-comprehensive proclamation, "Behold, I make all things new." The other is that word "white," not the cold, pallid white that may mean death, but the flashing white, as of sunshine upon snow, the radiant white that means purity smitten by Divinity, and so blazing up into lustre that dazzles. There are "white thrones," and "white robes," and "white horses," and all these express one and the same thing, that one element in the newness of the "new name" is spotless purity and supernal radiance. Here, at the best, our whiteness is but blackness washed, and on the road to be cleansed.

The "new name" means new joys, which, in comparison with the gladnesses of earth, shall be like the difference between the blazing sunshine on an ordinary June day, and the dim transient gleams of an ordinary frosty December day. Here and now, we know joy and sorrow as a double star, one bright and the other dark, which revolve round one center, and with terrible swiftness take each other's places. But there, "thou makest them drink of the river of thy pleasures," and no longer shall we have to speak of them as being—

> Like the snowflakes on the river,
> A moment white, then gone for ever

but as sealed with the solemn seal of perpetuity, and clarified into the utmost height of purity, and calm with the majesty of a divine tranquillity, after the pattern of His joy that was full and abode an undisturbed unchanging blessedness.

There is another promise in one of the other letters, which is often read as if it covered the same ground as that of Rev. 2:17 but, in reality, it is different, though closely connected. In the next chapter we read, in the 12th verse, "Him that overcometh will I make a pillar in the temple of My God, and I will write upon him"—perhaps we may carry the metaphor of the pillar onwards into this clause, and think of *it* as inscribed with what follows—"the name of My God"—in token of ownership—"the name of the city of My God, which is the 'new Jerusalem' "—in token of citizenship—"and I will write upon him My 'new name'."

What is this "new name" of Christ's? Obviously, remembering the continual use of the word "name" in Scripture, the new name of Jesus is a revelation of His character, nature, and heart; a new manifestation of Himself to the glad eyes of those that loved Him, when they saw Him amidst the darkness and the mists of earth, and so have been honored to see Him more clearly amidst the radiances of the glories of heaven.

Only remember that when we speak of a "new name" of Christ's as being part of the blessedness of the future state to which we may humbly look forward, it is no antiquating of the old name. Nothing will ever make the Cross of Jesus Christ less the center of the revelation of God than it is to-day. The world sweeps on, and when the great ages of eternity have come, there will sink beneath the horizon of the past many a tall column that stands high and flashes lights from its summit to-day. But no distance onwards, nor any fresh illumination, will ever pale the light that shines from the earthly manifestation and bitter Passion of the Christ, the Revealer of God. We antiquate none of that because we look for a deeper understanding of what it reveals when we come to the loftier station of the heavens. And as for earth, so for heaven. The paradox of this Apostle is true, and Christ Himself will say to us then, "Brethren! I write no new commandment unto you, but an old commandment which ye had from the beginning. Again, a new commandment write I unto you, because the darkness is past the true light now shineth." But the new name is the new name of the old Christ.

Then what is the inscription of that name upon the conqueror? It is not merely the manifestation of the revealed character of Jesus in new beauty, but it is the manifestation of His ownership of His servants by their transformation into His likeness, which transformation is the consequence of their new vision of Him. "I will write upon him My new name," is but saying, in other words, "The new revelation of My character, which he shall receive, will be stamped upon his character, and he shall become like Myself." It is but putting into picturesque form what this same Apostle said in more abstract words when he declared, "When He shall be manifested, we shall be like Him, for we shall see Him as He is." Here we see Him as He has become for our sins, and the imperfect vision partially works likeness; there seeing Him as He is, we become as He is. The name is inscribed upon the beholder as the sun makes an image of itself on the photographic plate. If thou wouldest see Christ, thou must be as Christ; if thou wouldest be as Christ, thou must see Christ. "We all, with unveiled faces, mirroring," as a glass does, "the glory of the Lord, are changed into the same image."

So, then, our "new name" is Christ's new name stamped upon us. On the day of the bridal of the Lamb and the Church, the bride takes her Husband's name, and all who love Him and pass into His sweet presence in the heavens are named by His new name because they partake of His life. "He that is joined to the Lord is one spirit," and Christ's name is his name.

Notice the blessed secret of this new name.

"No man knoweth it save he that receiveth it." Of course not. There is only one way to know the highest things in human experience, and that is by possessing them. Nobody can describe love, sorrow, gladness, so as to awaken a clear conception of them in hearts that have never experienced them. And so poetry goes side by side with man through the ages, and is always foiled in its efforts, and feels that it has not yet reached the heart of the mystery that it tries to speak. Its words only awaken *memories* in those who have already known the things, and you can no more impart a knowledge of the deepest human experiences to men who have not experienced them than you can describe an odor or a taste. That is eminently true about religion, and it is most of all true about that perfect future state.

"No man knoweth it saving he that receiveth it." Well, then, when we go one inch beyond the utterances of Him that does know—that is, Jesus Christ—then we get into dreams and errors. And we can no more conceive that future life, apart from the utterances of our Lord, either from His own lips or through His inspired servants, than an unborn child can construct a picture of the world that it has never seen. A chrysalis, lying under ground, would know about as much of what it would be like, when it had got its wings and lived upon sweetness, and blazed in the sunshine, as a man when he lets his imagination attempt to construct a picture of another life. I abjure all such. I try to speak plain inferences from manifest certitudes of Scripture. And I beseech you to remember that for us the curtain is the picture, and that the more detailed and precise descriptions of that future life are, whether in popular religious books or elsewhere, the more sure they are to be wrong. Death keeps his secret well, and we have to pass his threshold before we know what lies beyond.

But more than that. That same blessed mystery lies round about the name of each individual possessor, to all but himself. That sounds a questionable joy. We know how sad it is to be unable to speak our deepest selves to our dearest ones, and feel as if no small part of that future blessedness lay in the thought of the power of absolute self-impartation down to the very roots of our being. And I do not think that my text denies that. The New Testament teaches us that the redeemed shall "be manifested," and shall be able, therefore, to reveal themselves to the very secret foundations of their being. And yet each eye shall see its own rainbow, and each will possess in happy certitude of individual possession a honeyed depth of sweet experience which, after all glad revelation, will remain unrevealed, the basis of the being, the deep foundation of the blessedness. Just as we shall know Christ perfectly, and bear His new name inscribed upon our foreheads, and yet *He* has "a name which no man knoweth but He Himself," so the mystery of each redeemed soul will still remain impenetrable to others. But it will be a mystery of no painful darkness, nor making any barrier between ourselves and the saints whom we love.

Rather it is the guarantee of an infinite variety in the manner of possessing the one name. All the surrounding diamonds that are set about the central blaze shall catch the light on their faces, and from one it will come golden, and from another violet, and another red, and another flashing and pure white. Each glorified spirit shall reveal Christ, and yet the one Christ shall be manifested in infinite variety of forms, and the total summing up of the many reflections will be the image of the whole Lord. As the old Rabbis named the angels that stood round the throne of God by divers names, expressive of the divers forms which the one Divine Presence assumed to them, and called one Gabriel, "God, my Strength"; and another Uriel, "God, my Light"; and another Raphael, "God, the Healer"; and another Michael, "who is like God"; so, as we stand about the Christ, we shall diversely manifest His one glory, one after this manner and another after that.

Lastly, note the giving of the new name to the victors. The language of my text involves two things: "To him that overcometh" lays down the conditions; "Will I give" lays down the cause of the possession of the "new name"—that is to say, this renovation of the being, and efflorescence into new knowledges, activities, perfections, and joys, is only possible on condition of the earthly life of obedience, and service, and conquest. It is no arbitrary bestowment of a title. The conqueror gets the name that embodies his victories, and without them a man cannot receive it. It is not dying that fits a man for heaven, or makes it possible for God to give it him. God would give it him if He could, but God cannot. His limitation, inseparable from His being, and from the nature of the gift, lies here—"To him that overcometh," and only to him, "will I give." The name corresponds to the reality, and in heaven men are called what they are.

But while the conquering life here is the condition of the gift, it is none the less a gift. That heavenly blessedness is not the necessary consequence of earthly faithfulness. It is not a case of evolution, but of bestowal by God's free love in Christ. The power by which we conquer is His gift. The life which He crowns is His gift, and when He crowns it is His own grace in them which He crowns. "The gift of God is eternal life."

So, here is the all-important truth for us all. "This is the victory that overcometh the world, even our faith;" and that faith is victorious in idea and germ as soon as it begins to abide in a man's heart. If he were to die the one moment, having the moment before yielded himself to Christ in faith, he would be a victor, and capable of the crown, which God will give to those who overcome, whether they have fought for the twelve hours of the conflict or but for a moment at its close. This great promise is held out to each of us. It opens before us the sure prospect of blessedness, progress, power and joy, shoreless and infinite, unspeakable after all speech, and certain as yesterday. Either that prospect is before us, or its dark opposite. We shall either conquer by Christ's faith and in Christ's strength, and so receive His divine name, or else be beaten by the world and "the flesh and the devil," and so bear the image of our conquerors. Make your choice that you will be of those who, having got the victory over the beast and his image and the number of his name, stand at last on the sea of glass with the harps of God, and sing a song of thanksgiving to Him by whom they have overcome, and whose image and name they bear.

ON THE WINNING SIDE

Only let your conversation be as it becometh the Gospel of Christ: that whether I come and see you, or else be absent, I may hear of your affairs, that yet stand fast in one spirit with one mind striving together for the faith of the Gospel: and in nothing terrified by your adversaries.

(PHIL. 1:27, 28)

WE READ in the Acts of the Apostles that Philippi was a chief city and a colony. Now, the connection between a Roman colony and Rome was a great deal closer than that between an English colony and England. It was, in fact, a piece of Rome on alien soil. The colonists and their children were Roman citizens; their names were inscribed on the list of Roman tribes; they were governed by their own magistrates, not by the provincial authorities; the code to which they owed obedience was the law of Rome, not of the locality which they inhabited.

Now, no doubt many of the Philippian Christians, like the Apostle himself, shared in these privileges, and to them the idea of dwelling in a community to which they were less closely bound than to the mother city beyond the sea was quite familiar. They lived in Philippi—they belonged to Rome. And it is that idea which gives the special coloring to the first words of my text, which our translation, unfortunately, entirely obliterates, for the rendering of the phrase which is expressed in our Bible: "Let your conversation be," is really: "Play the citizen; act as a citizen."

"Conversation" was an inadequate rendering, even when our version was made; it has become more inadequate now when the word has dwindled to express, not, as it did then, conduct, but talk. But what the Apostle means is not do your civic duties as citizens as becomes the Gospel, though a great many of us would be all the better for laying that exhortation to heart, but the quality which he desires to stimulate in all Christian people, the sense of belonging to, is that of the mother country, the mother city above the stars. And that idea is worked out, as it seems to me, in the subsequent clauses. "Let your conversation be," or, as I would read it, "play the citizen," "as becometh the Gospel of Christ." You have got the city's laws, but these are your code. The outlying colonists on the borders of Rome's empire received their little bit of land on condition of "keeping the marches," and, where possible, pushing forward the frontier. And so, says Paul, "Act the citizen, striving together for the faith of the Gospel." The isolated post on the frontier—in some block-house or camp—felt the empire was at their backs, and so they were not afraid of the hosts of barbarians in front. And, so says Paul, "in nothing terrified by your adversaries."

First, I would say: Keep fresh the sense of belonging to the mother country, the mother city. Paul was writing to Philippi, where, it was a distinction to say: "I am a Roman," and he was writing from Rome where, even in the degenerate days of Nero, he could see how the consciousness of citizenship gave dignity and became almost a religion; and it is that kind of sense that he desires to stimulate in all of us professing Christians.

There is a community, a civic community, in existence at this moment, to which we belong. There is in existence the solemn and august community to which every Christian man and woman, in the measure of his or her Christianity doth truly belong. For if you are living, however imperfectly and tremulously, by faith in, and obedience to, Jesus Christ the Saviour, your true affinities are yonder, and not here. The lives of Christian men on earth, and the lives of "the spirits of just men made perfect," who make up part of the inhabitants of that great city, are one in essence, however different in degree of approximation to that which makes them live; for the source is the same, and the life of the saint on earth, however imperfect his sanctity, and however much he is embarrassed with earth, is fundamentally derived from the same source as the life of the perfect spirits who have longest drunk in the fullest vitality from Him who is the Life and the Light of all who live or "sleep"; one in source, one in essential characteristics, one in scope and direction! Therefore—

> One army of the living God,
> At His command we bow.

And the men who belong to Christ by rudimentary faith, love and often imperfect and broken obedience thereby are knit by closer bonds to the perfect spirits beyond the sea than they are to the men that stand beside them in the counting-house or sit beside them on the benches of the University or work beside them in the workshop. Our affinities, if we are Christ's, are yonder and not here.

And so, Grace, like almost all the great capitals of the world, has a suburb across the river—a Rome on the other side of the Tiber. We are there and they are yonder, but the municipality is one—

> Though now divided by the stream,
> The narrow stream of death!

And so, our work is cut out for us. The thing to do is to try to keep vivid that consciousness that "here we have no continuing city." It is no painful consciousness if you go the right way to work to produce it, and let it be the result of the thrilling and glad consciousness that you belong to Jesus Christ and the city that is His. And remember that that sense of detachment is by no means contradictory to, rather it is stimulative of, the interest, energy and effort in regard to the duties of this present. It is nonsense when people talk—and they sometimes do talk as if they believed it—it is nonsense to say that when I let in the light of the other world into my little low chamber here below, I diminish the importance of what is there. I illuminate it. Shelley talks about "the many-colored dome of glass that stains the white radiance of eternity." It is the "white radiance of eternity" streaming through "the many-colored dome of glass" that gives all the luster to its color. And so we magnify the things of Time when we connect them with the things of eternity, and the suburb across the river looks less mean and forlorn when we think that it belongs to the great municipality, across the border. "So, keep fresh the consciousness of belonging to the mother city, and let the sense, "here we have no continuing city, but we seek one to come," not be the bitter fruit of the sad experience of earth's transciency, but the joyful result of seeking the city "which hath the foundations."

Secondly, live by the city's laws, act the citizen "as becometh the Gospel." Not the provincial code demands your allegiance but the Imperial rescripts; and if we belong to, and have our affinities, and the roots of our being on the other side of the river, then we shall take our commands from thence, and it will be true of us what was said to the heathen king, by their enemies, of the Jews—that they were a people of whose laws were "different from all the peoples that be upon the earth." Worthily, "as becometh the Gospel."

The Gospel is not a mere message of deliverance, but it is a canon of conduct; it is not a theology to be accepted only, but it is ethics to be lived. It is not to be believed only, but it is to be taken into the life as a guide.

Have you realized that when you say, "He loved me and gave Himself for me," you are thereby laying down the supreme and sovereign law for what you are to do and what you are to be? Have you realized that in the story of the cross there is an Imperial law for all believers, or do you think of it only as promising you—you don't know exactly why impunity,—you don't know exactly what that means—for your sins? Act the citizen "as becometh the Gospel of Christ." There is the perfect ideal of humanity in the life and in the death of your Redeemer. Don't say that death is inimitable, and can never be repeated while the world stands. That is quite true—thank God it *is* true! It cannot be repeated because it does not need to be repeated. but it is not true that you cannot shape your lives so as to be partakers of His sufferings, and to know the fellowship of them, before you know, or simultaneously with your knowing, "the power of His resurrection." For there, not only the gracious gentleness, and weak wisdom, and serene composure, and fuller submission of the life, but in the death for men that hated Him, stands the pattern for all men's lives. And if you and I are going to act the citizen "as becometh the Gospel," we shall have to copy—with reverence be it spoken, and yet assuredly be it spoken—"the dying of the Lord Jesus," "that the life also of Christ may be manifest in our mortal body."

And from out of that Gospel come, streaming with vivifying energy, all the mighty motives which will make it possible for our conduct to be conformed to that great Pattern. Not only the ideal of conduct but the impulses and the motives and the powers to realize that ideal are laid up most abundantly in the Gospel of Jesus Christ, and pour out from it into every heart that wills to receive them with the most electric and stimulating energy.

Then, don't forget that a part of thus living according to the city's laws is that you don't live according to the laws of the community in which you are visibly present. "This did not I because of fear of the Lord," must always play a large part in the regulation of the conduct of men whose affinities are beyond the bounds of this visible diurnal sphere. We report to headquarters. This is conceived to be a distinction to the officials of our widely-scattered empire. It is a feather in a man's cap when he has not to send up his statements to the governor of the nearest colony, but straight to Downing street. And you and I don't need to mind what A., B. or C. say about us. "With me it is a very small matter to be judged of you or of men's judgment." Why should I mind about that when "He that judgeth me is the Lord"? "Wherefore we labor, that, whether present or absent, we may be well-pleasing to Him," nor know nothing more fair than is the smile upon Thy face. Live by the laws of the city, and let the tongues of the suburb wag as they will.

Thirdly, my advice or request, following the Apostle's lead, is *fight for its advancement*. "That I may hear of your affairs, that ye stand fast in one spirit"—there is the unity of successful resistance, opposing all the assaults that may be made upon you—"in one mind striving together for the faith of the Gospel"—there is the unity of conjoint aggressive action. The colonists had to stand a barrier against the sometimes on-rushing tide of barbarian invasion, but they had also to hitch forward the frontier when they could. And so we have not only to "stand fast," but we have to "strive" for the advancement—in ourselves and in the world—of the faith. And it is no easy matter to do that in a day like this, when there are so many occasional and incidental antagonists to faith, in addition to the permanent ones which belong to human nature always and everywhere.

But note, how strongly the Apostle here strikes the chord of unity as the one condition of either successful resistance or prosperous aggression. "In one spirit, with one mind, striving together for the faith of the Gospel." I don't speak about the wider vision, which lies to some of us so tragically, apparently, unattainable, when Christian men will understand who their brother is, and who their enemy is, and when all Christian people shall be drawn together in a mutual comprehensiveness which, if it does not include, at least does not allow forms to isolate or separate. But I would say that you will never do any good in your Church, unless you endeavor—not in the sense of a feeble attempt which is not sure of success, but in the sense of a strenuous dead-lift determination that it shall be so—to "keep the unity of the spirit in the bond of peace."

Fourthly: *Be sure of victory.* "In nothing terrified by your adversaries." The Apostle uses a strong metaphor which is drawn from the shying of a horse from some obstacle that it does not understand. You are not to start aside, or be frightened by nervous, panic fears, and so be diverted from your course.

A great many Christians seem to be half-ashamed of their Christianity, or of the parts of it that the world thinks offensive, and who don't like to state their views in any very definite and strong fashion, and in fact mumble "I believe" as if it were an apology rather than a creed. And I want you, to be sure that you are going to win. The certainty that I am going to do it has a wonderful knack of fulfilling itself. You be sure of success. And you have a good reason to be sure. You have all the powers of the city on the other side of the river there at your back, and you have got some of them in your heart, and you will succeed if you use what you possess. You remember the old story, which has been repeated in many another beleaguered city, of the men of Lucknow holding grimly by the ruins, and with a shoreless sea of cruel savagery, mutinous and raging for their blood round them; and they heard through the air the faint notes that told them relief was coming. And, in this very letter, our Apostle says, using something of the same metaphor, and using the same expression as in my text: "Our citizenship is in heaven, from whence also we look for the Lord Jesus Christ as Saviour." He is coming, and presently He will have come, and the black-visaged rebel rout will be helter-skelter on the horizon. "Blessed are they that wash their robes, that they may have right to the tree of life, and may enter in through the gates into the city."

LIVING IN
THE LIGHT OF VICTORY

Wherefore gird up the loins of your mind, be sober, and hope to the end for the grace that is to be brought unto you at the revelation of Jesus Christ.
(I PETER 1:13)

CHRISTIANITY HAS transfigured hope and invested it with a new importance, by giving it a new world in which to expatiate and new guarantees on which to rest. Like all our faculties, it is ennobled by coming in touch with Jesus Christ, then ceases to be a mere dream of uncertain pleasant possibilities and becomes a certain anticipation of certain good. In our conventional religious phraseology we pit grace against good, but the Apostle Peter places them on top of each other, like two triangles superimposed one upon the other; they are absolutely coterminous, and they cover precisely the same ground. The apostle had just been speaking of an inheritance incorruptible and undefiled, and that fades not away; he had just been speaking of the praise and honor and glory which were to be found at the appearing of Jesus Christ; he had just been speaking about the salvation of our souls which was the end of our faith: and whatever is included in these three phrases of the preceding context is equally included in this phrase, "The grace that is to be brought unto us."

People generally talk about grace as being the earnest of the inheritance. Here it is set forth as the whole purpose, the whole fullness of the future Christian possession. People generally, as I said, pit grace against glory. Here it is the very same thing as the praise and honor and glory which are to be found at the appearing— mark the parallelism of expression—at the appearing of Jesus Christ. We usually talk about grace as being shorthand for the whole sum of the supplies which Christian men receive, Divinely communicated as they are approximating towards the final salvation. Here it is identical with that salvation.

Now, I want you to mark what comes from this coalescence, as it were, or flowing together of these two ideas of the grace and the glory. Well, there comes one thing from it, and that is that away out into the infinite depths of that future, and away up into the invisible heights of that advance towards the likeness and the blessedness of God, the same thing lies at the foundation of all of this that first lay at the foundation of the tremulous hope of the poor penitent when he first caught sight of the cross of Christ, and scarcely dare to believe that in it his salvation was made sure.

There is an old hymn that used to be more sung when I was a boy than it is now, and some of the older members of this congregation will remember the resounding energy with which we used to sing it to an old-fashioned tune that has gone out of practice:

> Grace all the work shall crown
> To everlasting days;
> It lays in heaven the topmost stone,
> And well deserves the praise.

All the fullness of glory is the gift of grace, free, undeserved, spontaneous love, and we shall never through the ages of eternity cease to be undeserving of the smallest drop of the abundance with which we are drenched and saturated. Grace is glory.

And there is another thing, and that is that the same coalescence of these two ideas may well suggest to us the absolute homogeneousness of the Christian life in its furthest reaches of sublimity and strangeness, and in its infantile beginnings and feeblenesses here below. And there are great differences, and the differences are so deep, as well as so great and so radical, as that imagination fails in forecasting them, and it is a very profitless task to try to do it. But it is far better to remember that, however great may be the differences, the identity is far deeper and more important, and that the difference between the glory of the heavens and the grace here is but—if I may use such a violent figure—like the difference between a picture seen in the shadow, where all the lights are feeble, and the same carried out into the sunlight, where all the colors blaze. Grace is glory in the bud, and glory is grace in the fruit.

Then there is another point which Peter lays upon our hearts here. Mark the words, "the grace that is to be brought." Now, that perhaps most pedantically but accurately rendered would be, "the grace that is being brought to you." "Being brought"—it is on the road, the motion has already begun which will land it here, if I might take such an illustration. The angels that bear it have already set out on the road. Peter is so absolutely sure of its coming that he says, Why, it has started already, and it is coming nearer, and nearer, and nearer every instant, and presently what was a speck will become a disc, and what was a disc will become a ball of light, and what was a ball of light will become the face, the face of the Christ that appears, and it will be ringed round with the halo into which all them that love His appearing will be sucked, the grace that is being brought to it. They tell us that there are great suns away out in the infinitudes of space whose beams set out before a man was on the earth, and their rays have not yet impinged upon any eye, but they are on the road. And so this is the grace that is being brought, is in process of being wafted towards us. And that grace, that glory, that approximating brightness, is all coming in the revelation of Jesus Christ, and when He comes it comes. We know that when He shall appear we shall be like Him, for we shall see Him as He is. When Christ who is our life shall appear, then shall we also appear with Him in glory. You take these three thoughts—with Christ, like Christ, glory in Christ—never mind about all the rest. There are plenty of symbols, and there are negations in abundance, blessed negations which help us to body forth something of that future; but I profoundly believe that the less we clog our imaginations with physical theories of another life or details of that sort, the more sanely and soundly our imaginations will work on the question. Why, the fully artistic and highly-colored pictures that you put into your children's hands nowadays do not do half as much for them to stimulate them and to enable them to body out the scenes as the rude, wretched old things that we used to have when I was a child; and the less you paint, the more you will perceive the veil is the curtain. Richard Baxter, who knew as much about such things as most people, said in that great hymn of his:

> My knowledge of that life is small,
>   The eye of faith is dim,
> But 'tis enough that Christ knows all,
>   And I shall be with Him.

So much, then, for my first point. And now to the second—the duty, the imperative duty of Christian hope. Well, you say, that is a duty I never thought of. No, a great many Christian people never did think of it as being a duty. They say to themselves, "I cannot command my feelings." No, you cannot command your feelings, but

Living in the Light of Victory

I will tell you what you can command. The direction of your thoughts and feelings will follow the thought, depend on it, and it is as much a Christian man's duty, or a Christian woman's duty for that matter, to cultivate this clear hope as it is to cultivate any other Christian grace.

You remember in the Epistle to the Hebrews the writer has just been commending the people for their certain forms of Christian beneficence in which they were evidently abundant, and he goes on to say—let me put it into more modern English than the New Testament—he goes on to say, "I wish very much that you would be as diligent in trying to strengthen your Christian hope as you are in showing kindness to the Christian brethren." We desire that every one of you do show the same diligence—the same diligence as what? The same diligence as he had been commending them for showing in reference to ministering to the necessities of the saints. I wish you had as much care to cultivate Christian emotions as some of you have to do what is called Christian work. The work would be a great deal better if the emotions were more looked after. The cultivation of this onward look as a part of the Christian life will not weaken our energy down here in our daily life, of course not! Why, the higher the cliff from which the water falls, the more electricity will it generate to drive any wheels that you may put in its way; and the more a man lives above the world, with the bigger impact will he come down upon it and leave a dint and make a mark that shows his presence.

You go and look upon some wide-stretching bit of moorland with a great sky over it. It is dull, featureless, uninteresting, ugly. Sweep away the veil and let the blue heaven be visible, and every little tuft of heather flashes into beauty, and every dark, sullen bit of water in the big bog reflects the blue of the heaven, and a transformation has come over the whole thing. Life is great when it is looked upon in connection with the heavens, but when we strike out the hope, life becomes "a tale told by an idiot, full of sound and fury signifying nothing." Cultivate this hope as a duty if you want to do energetic work in the world.

But let me remind you that the imperative duty here is not only to hope, but to hope perfectly. And what goes to the perfection of hope? Two things—certainty and continuity. Certainty! A great poet, in one of his sweetest words, has spoken about "hopes and fears that kindle hope, an undistinguishable throng."

But there are fears that kill hope, and the definition of it is an anticipation which is obviously less than certainty. But Jesus Christ comes to us, and His "Verily, verily" enables us to take for our word in contemplating that future, not "Peradventure," but "Verily, verily." It is something to have a hope which is as certain as memory—more certain—and to have a future which is as unchangeable as the calm and determined past. And you can get that if you like, if you will take the assurance that Jesus in His words and in His Person—gives us, that where He is there will also His servant be.

But there is also another element in the perfection of hope, and that is continuity. That is where I suppose we must all confess that we break down. They tell us that there is a mountain in the swampy districts of Central Africa that people only see for an hour or two in the morning, and as soon as the mists drawn up by the sun rise from the swamps around about it, it is shrouded in cloud. That is like the hopes of a great many Christian people gleaming out now and then, and then shrouded, and shrouded by the mist that comes up from the undrained swamps. Hope perfectly!

Living in the Light of Victory

Now, this insisting on the duty of Christian hope is a lesson very much needed in this day. I do not know what your experience is but my suspicion is that we hear very little from the pulpit about the future life, and that anticipation of the future as a factor in our Christian lives and as an element in our Christian experience is much less than it used to be in our fathers' time. That has come partly from the prominence, much to be rejoiced over in many respects, which the social side of Christianity and its effects on the present world have had in recent days, and it has come partly from the spread of the so-called scientific spirit, which wants verification for everything before it believes it; and it comes, I believe, a great deal more than either from the weakening of the Christian life in our churches. And so I venture to press upon you, that one of the primary duties of the Christian man, and one of the most important of the elements in his Christian growth, is the cultivation of this Christian hope.

That brings me to my last word, and that is the culture or discipline ancillary to this Christian hope: "girding up the loins of your mind." A loose robe tangles a man's feet, trips him up if he tries to run, gets caught in the thorns, may be laid hold of by an enemy that wants to drag him back, and every toil, and every travel, and every battle you have got to tuck it up well from the waist. It is a very Eastern metaphor. May I substitute an English vulgarism for it which means precisely the same thing?—Pull yourselves together, that is to say, you will get no radiance of Christian hope in your lives without making a great effort for it. A sixpence held close to a man's eye will shut out the sun from him. There is only a certain quantity of energy and power of attention given to us, and if we direct it all in one quarter there will be

VICTORY IN FAILURE

none of it left for the other. You may take all the water out of the river and turn it in by a sluice into a miller's lake to grind his corn, and then the bed of the stream is left empty, and that is what a great many of us do. "Gird up the loins of your mind"; make the effort, for without the effort you will never rise into the great region of this hope.

And "being sober"—which, of course, I need not say covers a much wider ground than the prevailing vice of England has made the word cover in our experience—self-control, keeping a tight hand upon inclinations, and, if I may use a very unfashionable word, "lusts." There is nothing has such a power of dimming all the experiences of a Christian life, all the blessed ones, such as communion and hope, as the smallest indulgence in sin. Why, many a night some little film of cloud altogether invisible comes creeping across the sky, and however filmy and thin it may be there is substance enough in it to blot out the stars, and make a black place where planets were a moment before, and you only know that there is a cloud because you do not see the stars. And so the reason why in so many of our lives the great lights so often are eclipsed is because we are indulging in some ungoverned passion, or inclination, which leads us into sin. And, on the other hand, they have found out now that if you take a sensitive plate, and so arrange it in the observatory as that it shall travel along with the travelling heavens, by long exposure you will get upon it images of stars that no telescope is ever able to reveal. So you keep yourselves by girding your loins, which is effort, and by being sober, which is self-control—you keep yourselves with your whole hearts open to the celestial influences, and on the black background there will, by degrees, come out the little sparklet which speaks of a great sun far away beyond.

You have got that faculty, that strange faculty, of calling things that are not as though they were, and painting on the blank dim curtain of the future the likenesses of possible good. Where did you get it from? What did you get it for? You got it mainly that you might bring into the poor earthly life the glories of the heavenly world, and into the uncertainties of human experience the certainties of a Divine promise.

Do not you degrade and imprison your faculty of hope, making it as so many of us do, like a blind Samson with its eyes put out, grinding in our prison-house, but see that you train it to enter within the veil, and to gaze at and to grasp the inheritance, incorruptible and undefiled, and that fadeth now away.

VICTORY OVER THE LAST ENEMY

To whom God would make known what is the riches of the glory of this mystery among the Gentiles, which is Christ in you, the hope of glory.

(COL. 1:27)

PAUL AFFIRMS THAT it is his privilege to unfold and proclaim a great divine mystery. On several occasions he speaks of such a mystery. What does he mean by it? how would we define it?

From an examination of the passages in which the word occurs, we are led to describe it as a secret of the Lord which the human heart longs and craves to penetrate, however much it may be baffled in its attempts to do so. Such a secret is involved in the question: Is man destined for immortality, or is he not?

During the ages which preceded that of Christ and His great Apostle, the question of man's destiny was indeed a mystery, dark and discouraging in the extreme. Human beings everywhere found themselves in existence, without its being a matter of their own choice at all. The lives which they lived were in general very degraded and miserable, while at the same time their dread of death was intense. Nevertheless they were often quite ready to inflict it on one another on the slightest provocation; but whether or not this was the case, they all, without exception, perceived it awaiting them, grim and inevitable; and they could not discern anything beyond it. It filled all the future with its murky and inevitable darkness, and made the present to them but the valley of its shadow.

The grandest of Greek intellects characterized Plato—he was the loftiest and noblest by far of the ancient philosophers, and he no doubt held that the soul of man, in virtue of its divine essence, is immortal, that is, destined to exist endlessly; but he could say no more; he could only add that a revelation on the subject was imperatively required. In the great days of Rome, long afterwards, Cicero accepted Plato's teaching on the subject of immortality, but Cicero's contemporary, Julius Cæsar, on the other hand, regarded death as personal extinction, and so did multitudes besides. The Elysian Fields and gloomy Tartarus, of which the mild Virgil wrote, were in those days esteemed as mere dreams of the poets, of the reality of which no guarantee had been given to men. Well might Paul say of the poor heathen, that when they sorrowed over the demise of their relatives and friends, they sorrowed as men who had no hope. It is from the heathen that we have inherited the blackness that is still associated with our funerals. Our melancholy on these occasions is but the modification of their despair.

Even Old Testament saints and prophets were sometimes without such a clear and definite vision of the future beyond the tomb, as our Lord shows us they might have enjoyed. "The grave cannot praise Thee; death cannot celebrate Thee," exclaims Hezekiah. "What profit is there in my blood when I go down to the pit?" asks the Psalmist. They did not understand that if we are God's even "death is ours." They might have known that when Jehovah declared Himself to be the God of Abraham, of Isaac, and of Jacob, He was the God, not of the dead—the annihilated—but of the living; but they did not. Their faith sustained them in the pursuit of righteousness, and made existence tolerable and hopeful to them; but the lives of the best of the Old Testament saints had but little indeed of the brightness and the bliss which may easily become, which ought to become, the inheritance of every one who is born into the light of the Gospel day.

It is our Lord whom we habitually and most gladly

Victory over the Last Enemy

regard as the Almighty, yet human conqueror of death and the grave. Well has it been said of Him that He has "brought life and immortality to light." His own resurrection from the dead is well substantiated as a fact of history, but that which puts it beyond challenge is the marvellous, the perfect way in which it harmonizes with every other fact of His sinless, self-sacrificing, Divine life. Having voluntarily submitted to death for our sakes, it absolutely accords with the fitness of things that He, the Holy One of God, should not have been permanently held like other men in its fell and icy grasp.

You will find, if you think of it, that it is not the miracle of the Resurrection which makes us believe in Christ, but that, on the contrary, it is our understanding what Christ was and is, our belief in Christ Himself, which makes us easily accept His resurrection. We perceive that such a good and glorious Being as He ought not to be, in the universe of a righteous God could not possibly have been, the helpless victim of evil; that in the very nature of things it must have been made manifest that evil could not crush Him, that its worst assaults were directed against Him in vain. It is the heavenly beauty, the God-like glory of His life, in short, which has dispelled for ever the awful horror, the deep darkness which, because of human sin, so closely associated themselves with human dissolution, and has enabled us most confidently to rely on His declaration: "He that believeth on Me shall never die."

See, moreover, how amply the promise of glory, honor, and immortality is embodied even in these two words, which it was one of the great objects of His life to put into our lips and hearts, "Our Father." From first to last He labored to constrain His countrymen to call that God, of whom in reality they were terribly afraid, by this most attractive and consoling name. Well may it be said of Him that He has shewed to us the Father.

Think of your own love and care for your children, and desire for their good, and readiness to forget and forgive their worst errors if they will only cease from them, and your disposition to sacrifice yourselves to deliver and aid them, if you would understand in a measure how Jesus Christ would have you yourselves regard the living God. If God is our Father, as Jesus Christ says, must He not, therefore, have destined us for immortality, and is it not evident that the way in which we are to make it our inheritance is to show that we are in very deed His children.

It is told of a good man, who did much by the beneficence of his life, and by the true apprehension of the spirit of the New Testament which he has manifested in his writings, to remove the unnecessary austerity which has hitherto characterized Scottish theology, that he once met a shepherd on the hills, and in his own kind and impressive way said to him: "Do you know the Father?" and that years afterwards the same shepherd met him and instantly said: "I know the Father now." Is it not madness indescribable, wickedness unspeakable, to think of being anything else than His trusting, obedient, happy children, who leave ourselves, our future, our all, most thankfully, most confidently in His hands?

Men in our day have been unusually successful in discovering those secrets of Nature which evidently God has intended that they should discover, in order that human progress may be ensured. Some of them, accordingly, have arrived at the conclusion that nothing is to be believed but what can be proved to be true by the rules which regulate physical research. They forget that this implies a tremendous assumption—namely, that there is nothing in the world but matter and its laws, which is just another way of making exactly the most unreasonable assertion that man can make, the assertion that the universe is a meaningless, and worse than useless, thing, and that there is no God. But there are rules which regulate research in the moral and spiritual sphere likewise, and by applying these rules we come to know all that we need to know, to be satisfied that a blessed immortality awaits us; we come to have life, and to have it more abundantly.

The natural, as distinguished from the revealed, proofs that immortality is the destined lot of man, which are usually brought forward are, however, to be regarded as indications that it awaits him, rather than positive proofs of it. They show immortality to be a likely, but not a certain, thing. They are, moreover, indications not at all obvious to those whom sin has made gross and blind, but only to those who in departing from evil have acquired what Scripture calls a "good understanding." They consist in such things as these—man's desire for continued existence, his horror of the very thought of annihilation, his capability of making indefinite progress in knowledge, in wisdom, and in goodness; the fact, on the one hand, that his life here is a most distressing and insoluble enigma if death is to him the end of all things; and, on the other, that faith in his immortality alone can invest him with true dignity and inspire him with lofty impulse; and that, in accordance with all this, every nation on the face of the earth, however benighted, has made belief in a spiritual world and in a future state of blessing or retribution a part of its religion.

What the text promises is not the knowledge that believers in Christ shall enjoy a glorified immortality—it is something far more than this. It asserts that the presence

VICTORY IN FAILURE

of Christ in the believer, by His Spirit, is the pledge, creates in him the hope, generates in him the assurance that everlasting bliss awaits him. It tells us that in proportion as we become like the man Christ Jesus in disposition and character, so do we come to know, so does God give us to know, that we will be with Christ, which means everything when we are done with this world. It puts us in the way of having eternal life, and rejoicing in the possession of it, of securing our personal immortality. That exactly is what it does.

It enables us practically, if not theoretically, to solve the great problem, to penetrate the great mystery, in so far as the problem, the great mystery, concerns ourselves.

When we are aware that we are out of Christ, and that Christ is out of us, we regard heaven as hopelessly beyond our reach; we cannot help doing so; we do so from an irresistible necessity of nature. Christ's doctrines do not inspire us with the hope of glory, because Christ's pure, sweet, right, spirit of mind does not find place in us. In such an unhappy case the great future presents an awfully dreary, a menacing, a black prospect to us, from the contemplation of which we shrink back to occupy ourselves with the little things of the present time, our buying and selling and passing pleasures, about which at last we get so keen that we forget it altogether. It is an ostrich policy indeed. For there, notwithstanding, the future awaits us irremovable, impassable, infinite, even when we are blindly trifling on the verge of it; and some day we find ourselves obliged to take our leap in the dark, and our friends and neighbors lose all sight and trace of us, and turn away from our grave to think of other things; and God knows what then, and we know, too, when it is too late.

But "Christ in us" not only enables us to face the

future, but to do so with expectation and joy. His Spirit dwelling in our hearts, and characterizing our lives, rendering true of us "the Beatitudes," enables us to look on the heavenly inheritance as ours. We find it our very "title deed" to it, a God-given charter of rights. It is in truth the Spirit of the Son which enables us to claim the privileges of the Son. To have "Christ in us" is to possess "the one thing needful," is to be authorized to call "the pearl of great price," worth all things else, our own.

We do not, as I have already said, merely argue that because "Christ is in us," therefore we may hope to enter into glory at last. Mere argument on religious subjects does very little indeed for any man. Striving to be Christ's in the spirit of our mind, and in the deeds of our life, God our Father fills our hearts with a humble, but strong and happy assurance that all is well with us now, and will be for ever well with us when we are done with out labors here. In this way are our souls sustained, made cheerful, by being made hopeful within us, and we ourselves qualified by our cheerfulness for ever higher, more arduous measures of holy work.

It must, therefore, be obvious to you that the more steadily and rapidly Christ is being formed in the believer, the stronger and brighter will his hopes of glory become. Not that he is to constitute himself, as he goes along, the perfect judge of his own actions, and of the measure of heavenly reward to which he is in consequence entitled, like a man manufacturing goodness by the piece and selling it. This is not the Christian method of attaining to the assurance of hope at all; but that the more humbly, prayerfully, and unselfishly he renders to "our Father," a child's simple, true, and unreserved obedience, the more richly will the Father Himself enable him to rejoice in His love, and in all that it can bestow. It is not we ourselves who come to judgment day conclusions respecting ourselves of a satisfactory nature, and thus ensure our peace; it is God who reveals Himself to us as "Father of mercies, and the God of all comfort," as an Apostle calls Him. During those seasons of our life, accordingly, when we know that sin is not disturbing, unsettling us; when we are aware that we are being sustained and helped in answer to our prayers, we cherish convictions of the truth of what Christ has revealed concerning the place which He is preparing for us, which no sophisms of the infidel are able to overthrow.

On the other hand, by falling from this spiritual height, through our own carelessness, or yielding to temptation, and not at all by learning to reason more acutely, we are led to doubt, if not the existence of heaven, at least our own right of inheritance in it. Let us therefore, "giving all diligence," add to our faith day by day all the virtues and graces of the Divine life, as we are exhorted to do, that so an entrance may be ministered to us "abundantly into the everlasting kingdom of our Lord and Saviour Jesus Christ."

But do you feel, notwithstanding, strongly constrained to reply: "We do not doubt but what you teach is true, but of what use is it to us? Dare any of us venture to think, far less affirm, that 'Christ is in us,' in even such as we?"

Let me ask: Do you really believe that it is a salvation which we cannot possibly make ours that the God of Love, our Father, offers us, and beseeches us to accept? You cannot believe any such horrible thing. Let me point out to you, also, that it is to human goodness that He asks you to attain; He does not require you to be

Victory over the Last Enemy

just now good angels, but good, truly good, men and women in the spheres of life in which He has placed you respectively. Is that totally impracticable?

Let me further point out to you that He offers effectually to help you in the accomplishment of this very work; "My grace," says He, "is sufficient for thee, for My strength is made perfect in weakness." Must it not, then, really be determined unbelief, deliberate preference for a life of sin, in one form or another, that makes a man say that goodness, the goodness which his own conscience, and not another's, tells him should characterize him, is unattainable? To say so is to show one's self absolutely wanting in that faith without which it is impossible to please God. Who dare say that "our Father" waits to condemn us for not being what He Himself refuses to help us to be? The assertion is mere profanity.

"To be like Christ; oh, how high above us! Oh, how far beyond us, His perfect goodness, His immaculate holiness!" do you still exclaim? We all can sympathize with that exclamation when we remember what Christ as a man was, and reflect on what we ourselves, in comparison with him, really are. But, notwithstanding, may we not have something of Christ, a little of Christ, in us through Christ's own loving help? This is the good work which Christ Himself begins in us; this is the work of the new creation which "our Father" expects us to cooperate in carrying on to its glorious consummation.

But consider for a moment what it is to have even something of Christ in us. It means that His meekness and gentleness are supplanting our hot haste and harshness, His humility our obstinate pride, His loving kindness our narrowness and selfishness, His faith our fears, His moral purity our readiness to condone sin; it means that we are indeed being renewed in the spirit of our mind after the image of Him that created us. But, again, do you cry "Alas! our many and great imperfections!"

God, let me remind you, is "our Father," and is very kind to all His little children, bears with their weaknesses, pardons their sins, and does to them and for them "exceedingly abundantly above all that they can ask or think," gives them all possible encouragement and help. It does not follow that we cannot cherish hope, even the very "hope of glory" because in the meantime we come so very far short of being in every respect like Christ. If we could complete and round off our whole being in a few years, if we could quickly and easily reach our destined goal, and see nothing beyond it, that would be an argument against our immortality. The insect that comes to maturity in a day dies in a day. We all have to make a beginning for eternity, and if in three score and ten years we lay firm and sure the foundation of that perfection after which we strive we may be profoundly thankful.

We must have a high ideal, even the very highest, nothing short of "God manifest in the flesh" Himself, although it should take us all eternity, as it will, to rise to its fullness. If we are striving in very deed to obey the "eleventh commandment" we have nothing to fear; we are striving to obey all the rest; we are on the road to glory. "Love," said Christ, "as I have loved you"; and you know how He loved the publican, and the Magdalene, and the dying robber, and the Samaritan, and the Pharisee, and the outcast Canaanite—accepted their penitence; dropped out of sight their evil; laid hold of what possibilities of good were still in them, and raised them to heavenly places beside Himself.

Let us then not be of the miserable number who increase evil by their foolish methods of dealing with it; but let us learn to overcome it with good, and the day will surely dawn when we will be privileged to leave all evil behind and beneath us, and to take our stand among the countless hosts of white-robed saints who surround the throne.

THE VICTORIOUS TOUCH

Jesus put forth His hand and touched him.
(MARK 1:41)

"He puts out his hand"

"BEHOLD THE SERVANT OF THE LORD" might be the motto of the Gospel of Mark, and "He went about doing good, and healing," the summing up of its facts. We have in Mark comparatively few of our Lord's discourses, none of His longer, and not very many of His briefer ones. It contains but four parables. This Evangelist gives no miraculous birth as in Matthew, no angels adoring there as in Luke, no gazing into the secrets of Eternity, where the Word, Who afterwards became flesh, dwelt in the bosom of the Father, as in John. He begins with a brief reference to the Forerunner, and then plunges into the story of Christ's life of service to man, and service for God.

In carrying out his conception the Evangelist omits many things found in the other Gospels, which involve the idea of dignity and dominion, while he adds to the incidents which he has in common with them not a few fine and subtle touches to heighten the impression of our Lord's toil and eagerness in His patient loving service. Perhaps it may be an instance of this that we find more prominence given to our Lord's touch.

Whatever the reason, Mark delights to dwell on Christ's touch. The instances are these—first, He puts out His hand, and "lifts up" Peter's wife's mother, and immediately the fever left her (i. 31), then, unrepelled by the foul disease, He lays His pure hand upon the leper, and the living mass of corruption is healed (i. 41); again, He lays His hand on the clammy marble of the dead child's forehead, and she lives (i. 41). Further, we have incidental statement that He was so hindered in His mighty works by unbelief that He could only lay His hands on a few sick folk and heal them (vi. 5).

We find next two remarkable incidents, peculiar to Mark, both like each other and unlike our Lord's other miracles. One is the gradual healing of that deaf and dumb man whom Christ took apart from the crowd, laid His hands on him, thrust His fingers into his ears as if He would clear some impediment, touched his tongue with saliva, said to him, "Be opened"; and the man can hear (vii. 34). And the other is, the gradual healing of a blind man whom our Lord again leads apart from the crowd, takes by the hand, lays His own kind hands upon the poor sightless eyeballs, and with singular slowness of progress effects a cure, not by a leap and a bound as He generally does, but by steps and stages; tries it once and finds partial success, has to apply the curative process again and then the man can see (viii. 23).

In addition to these instances there are two other incidents. Mark alone records for us the fact that He took little children in His arms, and blessed them. And it is Mark alone who records for us the fact that when He came down from the Mount of Transfiguration He laid His hand upon the demoniac boy, writhing in the grip of his tormentor, and lifted him up.

Whatever diviner and sacreder aspect there may be in these incidents, the first thing and in some senses the most precious thing in them is that they are the natural expression of a truly human tenderness and compassion.

Now we are so accustomed to look at all Christ's life down to its minutest events as intended to be a revelation of God, that we are sometimes apt to think about it as if His motive and purpose in everything was didactic. So an unreality creeps over our conceptions of Christ's life, and we need to be reminded that He was not always acting and speaking in order to convey instruction, but that words and deeds were drawn from Him by the play of simple human feelings. He pitied not only in order to teach us the heart of God, but because His own man's heart was touched with a feeling of men's infirmities.

We are too apt to think of Him as posing before men with the intent of giving the great revelation of the Love of God. It is the love of Christ Himself, spontaneous, instinctive, without the thought of anything but the suffering it sees, which gushes out and leads Him to put forth His hand to the outcast beggars, the blind, the deaf, the lepers. That is the first great lesson we have to learn from this and other stories—the swift human sympathy and heart of grace and tenderness which Jesus Christ had for all human suffering; and has to-day as truly as ever.

There is more than this instinctive sympathy taught by Christ's touch. But it is distinctly taught. How beautifully that comes out in the story of the leper! That wretched man had long dwelt in his isolation. The touch of a friend's hand or the kiss of loving lips had been long denied him. Christ looks on him, and before he reflects the spontaneous impulse of pity breaks through the barriers of legal prohibitions, and of natural repugnance, and leads Him to lay His holy and healing hand on His foulness.

True pity always instinctively leads us to seek to come near those who are its objects. A man tells his friend some sad story of his sufferings, and while he speaks, unconsciously his listener lays his hand on his arm and, by a silent pressure, tells his sympathy. So Christ did with these men—not only in order that He might reveal God to us, but because He was a man, and therefore felt ere He thought. Out flashed from his heart the swift sympathy, followed by the tender pressure of the loving hand—a hand that tried through flesh to reach spirit and come near the sufferer that it might succor and remove the sorrow.

Christ's pity is shown by His touch to have this true characteristic of true pity, that it overcomes disgust. All real sympathy does that. Christ is not turned away by the shining whiteness of the leprosy, nor by the eating pestilence beneath it; He is not turned away by the clammy marble hand of the poor dead maiden, nor by the fevered skin of the old woman gasping on her pallet. He lays hold on each, the flushed patient, the loathsome leper, the sacred dead, with the all-equalizing touch of a universal love and pity, which disregards all that is repellent and overflows every barrier and pours itself over every sufferer.

We have the same pity of the same Christ to trust to and to lay hold of today. He is high above us and yet bending over us; stretching His hand from the throne as truly as He put it out when here on earth; and ready to take us all to His heart, in spite of our weakness and wickedness, our failings and our shortcomings, the fever of our flesh and hearts' desires, the leprosy of our many corruptions, and the death of our sins—and to hold us ever in the strong gentle clasp of His divine, omnipotent, and tender hand. This Christ lays hold on us because He loves us, and will not be turned from His compassion by the most loathsome foulness of ours.

The Victorious Touch

And now take another point of view from which we may regard this touch of Christ: namely as the medium of His miraculous power.

There is nothing to me more remarkable about the miracles of our Lord than the royal variety of His methods of healing. Sometimes He works at a distance, sometimes He requires, as it would appear for good reasons, the proximity of the person to be blessed. Sometimes He works by a simple word: "Lazarus come forth!" "Peace be still!" "Come out of him!" sometimes by a word and a touch, as in the instances before us; sometimes by a touch without a word; sometimes by a word and a touch and a vehicle, as in the saliva that was put on the tongue, and in the ears of the deaf, and on the eyes of the blind; sometimes by a vehicle without a word, without a touch, without His presence, as when He said "Go wash in the pool of Siloam! and he washed and was clean." So the divine worker varies infinitely and at pleasure yet not arbitrarily but for profound, even if not always discoverable, reasons, the methods of His miracle-working power, in order that we may learn by these varieties of ways that He is tied to no way; and that His hand, strong and almighty, uses methods and tosses aside methods according to His pleasure, the methods being vitalized when they are used by His will, and being nothing at all in themselves.

The very variety of His methods, then, teaches us that the true cause in every case is His own bare will. A simple word is the highest and most adequate expression of that will. His word is all powerful: and that is the very signature of divinity. Of Whom has it been true from of old that "He spake and it was done, He commanded and it stood fast?" Do you believe in a Christ Whose bare will, thrown among material things, makes them all plastic, as clay in the potter's hands, whose mouth rebukes the demons and they flee, rebukes death and it looses its grasp, rebukes the tempest and there is a calm, rebukes disease and there comes health?

But this use of Christ's touch as apparent means for conveying His miraculous power also serves as an illustration of a principle which is exemplified in all His revelation, namely, the employment in the condescension to men's weakness, of outward means as the apparent vehicles of His spiritual power. Just as by the material vehicle sometimes employed for cure, He gave these poor sensebound natures a ladder by which their faith in His healing power might climb, so in the manner of His revelation and communication of His spiritual gifts, there is provision for the wants of us men, who ever need some body for spirit to make itself manifest by, some form for the ethereal reality, some "tabernacle" for the "sun."

"Sacraments," outward ceremonies, forms of worship are vehicles which the Divine Spirit uses in order to bring His gifts to the hearts and the minds of men. They are like the touch of the Christ which heals, not by any virtue in itself, apart from His will which chooses to make it the apparent medium of healing. All these externals are nothing, as the pipes of an organ are nothing, until His Breath is breathed through them, and then the flood of sweet sound pours out.

Do not despise the material vehicles and the outward helps which Christ uses for the communication of His healing and His life, but remember that the help that is done upon earth, He does it all Himself. Even Christ's touch is nothing, if it were not for His own will which flows through it.

The Victorious Touch

Consider Christ's touch as a shadow and symbol of the very heart of His work.

Go back to the past history of this man. Ever since his disease declared itself no human being had touched him. If he had a wife he had been separated from her; if he had children their lips had never kissed his, nor their little hands found their way into his hard palm. Alone he had been walking with the plague-cloth over his face, and the cry "unclean!" on his lips, lest any man should come near him. Skulking in his isolation how he must have hungered for the touch of a hand! Every Jew was forbidden to approach him but the priest, who, if he were cured might pass his hand over the place and pronounce him clean. And here comes a man Who breaks down all the restrictions, stretches a frank hand out across the walls of separation and touches him. What a reviving assurance of love not yet dead, must have come to the man as Christ grasped his hand, even if he saw in him only a stranger who was not afraid of him and did not turn from him!

But beside this thrill of human sympathy, which came hope-bringing to the leper, Christ's touch had much significance, if we remember that, according to the Mosaic legislation, the priest and the priest alone was to lay his hands on the tainted skin and pronounce the leper whole. So Christ's touch was a priest's touch. He lays His hand on corruption and is not tainted. The corruption with which He comes in contact becomes purity. Are not these really the profoundest truths as to His whole work in the world? What is it all but laying hold of the leper and the outcast and the dead—His sympathy leading to His indentification of Himself with us in our weakness and misery?

That sympathetic life-bringing touch is put forth once for all in His Incarnation and Death. "He taketh hold of the seed of Abraham," says the Epistle to the Hebrews, looking at our Lord's work under this same metaphor, and explaining that His laying hold of men was His being "made in all points like unto his brethren." Just as he took hold of the fevered woman and lifted her from her bed; or, as He thrust His fingers into the deaf ears of that poor man stopped by some impediment, so, in analogous fashion, He becomes one of those whom He would save and help. In His assumption of humanity and in His bowing of His head to death, we behold Him laying hold of our weakness and entering into the fellowship of our pains and of the fruit of sin.

Just as He touches the leper and is unpolluted, or the fever patient and receives no contagion, or the dead and draws no chill of mortality into His warm hand, so He becomes like His brethren in all things, yet without sin. Being found in the likeness of sinful flesh, He knows no sin, but wears His manhood unpolluted and dwells among men blameless and harmless, the Son of God, without rebuke. Like a sunbeam passing through foul water untarnished and unstained; or like some sweet spring rising in the midst of the salt sea, which yet retains its freshness and pours it over the surrounding bitterness, so Christ takes upon Himself our nature and lays hold of our stained hands with the hand that continues pure while it grasps us, and will make us purer if we grasp it.

Let your touch answer to His; and as He lays hold of us, in His incarnation and His death, let the hand of our faith clasp His outstretched hand, and though our hold be as faltering and feeble as that of the trembling, wasted fingers which one timid woman once laid on His

The Victorious Touch

garment's hem, the blessing which we need will flow into our veins from the contact. There will be cleansing for our leprosy, sight for our blindness, life driving out death from its throne in our hearts, and we shall be able to recount our joyful experience in the old Psalmist's triumphant strains—"He sent me from above, He laid hold upon me, he drew me out of many waters."

Finally we may look upon these incidents as being in a very important sense a pattern for us.

No good is to be done by any man to his fellows except at the cost of true sympathy which leads to identification and contact. The literal touch of your hand would do more good to some poor outcasts than much solemn advice, or even much material help flung to them as from a height above them. A shake of the hand might be more of a means of grace than a sermon, and more comforting than ever so many free breakfasts and blankets given superciliously.

And, symbolically, we may say that we must be willing to take those by the hand whom we wish to help; that is to say, we must come down to their level, try to see with their eyes, and to think their thoughts, and let them feel that we do not think our purity too fine to come beside their filth, nor shrink from them with repugnance, however we may show disapproval and pity for their sin. Much work done by Christian people has no effect, nor ever will have, because it has peeping through it a poorly concealed "I am holier than thou." An instinctive movement of repugnance has ruined many a well-meant effort.

Christ has come down to us, and has taken all our nature upon Himself. If there is an outcast and abandoned soul on earth which may not feel that Jesus has laid a loving and healing touch on him, Jesus is not the Saviour for the world. He shrinks from none, He unites Himself with all, therefore He is able to save to the uttermost all who come unto God by Him.

His conduct is the pattern and the law for us. A Church is a poor affair if it be not a body of people whose experience of Christ's pity and gratitude for the life which has become theirs through His wondrous making Himself one with them, compel them to do the like in their degree for the sinful and the outcast. Thank God! there are many in every communion who know that constraint of the love of Christ! But the world will not be healed of its sickness till the great body of Christian people awakes to feel that the task and honor of each of them is to go forth bearing Christ's pity certified by their own.

The sins of professing Christian countries are largely to be laid at the door of the Church. We are idle when we ought to be at work. We pass by on the other side when bleeding brethren lie with wounds gaping to be bound up by us. And even when we are moved to service by Christ's love, and try to do something for them and for our fellows, our work is often tainted by a sense of our own superiority, and we patronize when we should sympathize, and lecture when we should beseech.

We must be content to take lepers by the hand, if we would help them to purity, and to let every outcast feel the warmth of our pitying, loving grasp, if we would draw them into the forsaken Father's House. Lay your hands on the sinful as Christ did, and they shall recover. All your holiness and hope come from Christ's laying hold of you. Keep hold of Him, and make His great pity and loving identification of Himself with the world of sinners and sufferers, your pattern as well as your hope,

The Victorious Touch

and your touch, too, will have virtue. Keeping hold of Him Who has taken hold of us, you, too, may be able to say "Ephphatha, be opened," or to lay your hand on the leper and he shall be cleansed.

WHAT IT TAKES TO WIN

And Ittai answered the king and said: As the Lord liveth, and as my lord the king liveth; surely in what place my lord the king shall be, whether in death or life, even there also will thy servant be.

(II SAM. 15:21)

IT WAS THE DARKEST HOUR in David's life. No more pathetic page is found in the Old Testament than that which tells the story of his flight before Absalom. He is crushed by the consciousness that his punishment is deserved—the bitter fruit of the sin that filled all his later life with darkness. His courage and his buoyancy have left him. He has no spirit to make a stand or strike a blow. If Shimei runs along the hillside abreast of him, shrieking curses as he goes, all he says is: "Let him curse; for the Lord hath him."

So, heartbroken and spiritless, he leaves Jerusalem. And as soon as he has got clear of the city he calls a halt in order that he may muster his followers and see on whom he may depend. Foremost among the little band come 600 men from Gath—Philistines—from Goliath's city. These men, singularly enough, the king had chosen as his body-guard; perhaps he was not altogether sure of the loyalty of his own subjects, and possibly felt safer with foreign mercenaries, who could have no secret leanings to the deposed house of Saul. Be that as it may, the narrative tells us that these men had "come after him from Gath." He had been there twice in the old days, in his flight from Saul, and the second visit had extended over something more than a year. Probably during that period his personal attraction, and his reputation as a brilliant leader, had led these rough soldiers to attach themselves to his service, and to be ready to forsake home and kindred in order to fight beside him.

At all events here they are, "faithful among the faithless"

as foreign soldiers surrounding a king often are—notably, for instance, the Swiss guard in the French Revolution. Their strong arms might have been of great use to David, but his generosity cannot think of involving them in his fall, and so he says to them: "I am not going to fight; I have no plan. I am going where I can. You go back and 'worship the rising sun.' Absalom will take you and be glad of your help. And as for me, I thank you for your past loyalty. Mercy and peace be with you!"

It is a beautiful nature that in the depth of sorrow shrinks from dragging other people down with itself. Generosity breeds generosity, and this Philistine captain breaks out into a burst of passionate devotion, garnished, in soldier-fashion, with an unnecessary oath or two, but ringing very sincere and meaning a great deal. As for himself and his men, they have chosen their side. Whoever goes, they stay. Whatever befalls, they stick by David; and if the worst come to the worst they can all die together, and their corpses lie in firm ranks round about their dead king. David's heart is touched and warmed by their outspoken loyalty; he yields and accepts their service. Ittai and his noble six hundred tramp on, out of our sight, and all their households behind them.

First, look at the picture of that Philistine soldier, as teaching us what grand passionate self-sacrifice may be evolved out of the roughest natures.

Analyze his words, and do you not hear, ringing in them, these three things, which are the seed of all nobility and splendor in human character? First, a passionate personal attachment; then, that love, issuing as such love always does, in willing sacrifice that recks not for a moment of personal consequences; that is ready to accept anything for itself if it can serve the object of its devotion, and will count life well expended if it is flung away in

What It Takes to Win

such a service. And we see, lastly, in these words a supreme restful delight in the presence of him whom the heart loves. For Ittai and his men, the one thing needful was to be beside him in whose eye they had lived, from whose presence they had caught inspiration; their trusted leader, before whom their souls bowed down. So then his vehement speech is the pure language of love.

Now these three things—a passionate personal attachment, issuing in spontaneous heroism of self-abandonment, and in supreme satisfaction in the beloved presence—may spring up in the rudest, roughest nature. A Philistine soldier was not a very likely man in whom to find refined and lofty emotion. He was hard by nature, hardened by his rough trade; and unconscious that he was doing anything at all heroic or great. Something had smitten this rock, and out of it there came the pure refreshing stream. And so the weakest and the lowest, the roughest and the hardest, the most selfishly absorbed man and woman has lying in him and her, dormant capacities for flaming up into a splendor of devotion and magnificence of heroic self-sacrifice. A mother will do it for her child, and never think that she has done anything extraordinary; husbands will do such things for wives; wives for husbands; friends and lovers for one another. All who know the sweetness and power of the bond of affection know that there is nothing more gladsome than to fling one's self away for the sake of those whom we love. And the capacity for such love and sacrifice lies in all of us; prosaic, commonplace people as we are, with no great field on which to work out our heroisms; yet it is in us to love and give ourselves away thus if once the heart be stirred.

And lastly, this capacity which lies dormant in all of us, if once it is roused to action will make a man blessed and dignified as nothing else will. The joy of unselfish love is the purest joy that man can taste; the joy of perfect self-sacrifice is the highest joy that humanity can possess, and they lie open for us all.

And wherever, in some humble measure, these emotions are realized, there you get weakness springing up into strength, and the ignoble into loftiness. Astronomers tell us that, sometimes, a star that has shone inconspicuous, and stood low down in their catalogs as of fifth or sixth magnitude, will all at once flame out, having kindled and caught fire somehow, and will blaze in the heavens, outshining Jupiter and Venus. And so some poor, vulgar, narrow nature, touched by this Promethean fire of pure love that leads to perfect sacrifice, will "flame in the forehead of the morning sky," an undying splendor, and a light for ever more.

You have all that capacity in you, and you are all responsible for the use of it. What have you done with it? Is there any person or thing in this world that has ever been able to lift you up out of your self? Is there any magnet that has proved strong enough to raise you from the levels along which your life creeps? Have you ever known the thrill of resolving to become the bond-servant and the slave of some great cause not your own? Or are you, as so many are, like spiders living in the midst of your web, mainly intent upon what you can catch in it?

You have these capacities slumbering in you. Have you ever set a light to that inert mass of enthusiasm that lies in you? Have you ever woke up the sleeper? Look at Ittai, this rough soldier, and learn from him the lesson that there is nothing that so ennobles and dignifies a commonplace nature as enthusiasm for a great cause, or self-sacrificing love for a worthy heart.

"... unto God the things that are God's"

What It Takes to Win

Secondly these possibilities of love and sacrifice point plainly to God in Christ as their true object. "Whose image and superscription hath it?" said Christ, looking at the Roman *denarius* that they brought and laid on His palm. If the Emperor's head is on it, why, then, *he* has a right to it as tribute. And then He went on to say, "Render, therefore, unto Cæsar the things which are Cæsar's, and unto God the things that are God's." So there are things that have God's image and superscription stamped on them, and such are our hearts, our whole constitution and nature. As plainly as the penny had the head of Augustus on it, and therefore proclaimed that he was Emperor where it was current, so plainly does every soul carry in the image of God, the witness that He is its owner and that it should be rendered in tribute to Him.

And among all these marks of a divine possession and a divine destination printed upon human nature, none are plainer than this fact, that we can give ourselves away in the abandonment of a profound and all-surrendering love. That capacity unmistakably proclaims that it is destined to be directed towards God and to find its rest in Him. As distinctly as some silver cup, with its owner's initials and arms engraved upon it, declares itself to be "meet for the master's use," so distinctly does your soul, by reason of this capacity, proclaim that it is meant to be turned to Him in Whom alone all love can find its perfect satisfaction; for Whom alone it is supremely blessed and great to shed life itself: and Who only has the authority over our human spirits.

We are made with hearts that need to rest upon an absolute love; we are made with understandings that need to grasp a pure, a perfect, and, as I believe, paradoxical though it may sound, a personal Truth. We are made with wills that crave for an absolute authoritative command, and we are made with a moral nature that needs a perfect holiness. And we need all that love, truth, authority, purity, to be gathered into one, for the misery of the world is that when we set out to look for treasures we have to go into many lands and to many merchants to buy many goodly pearls. But we need One of great price, in which all our wealth may be invested. We need that One to be an undying and perpetual possession. There is One to Whom our love can ever cleave, and fear none of the sorrows or imperfections that make earthward-turned love a rose with many a thorn, One for Whom it is pure gain to lose ourselves, One Who is plainly the only worthy recipient of the whole love and self-surrender of the heart.

That One is God, revealed and brought near to us in Jesus Christ. In that great Savior we have a love at once divine and human. We have the great transcendent instance of love leading to sacrifice. On that love and sacrifice for us Christ builds His claim on us for our hearts, and our all. Life alone can communicate life; it is only light that can diffuse light. It is only love that can kindle love; it is only sacrifice that can inspire sacrifice. And so He comes to us, and asks that we should just love Him back again as He has loved us. He first gives Himself utterly for and to us, and then asks us to give ourselves wholly to Him. He first yields up His own life, and then He says: "He that loseth his life for my sake shall find it." The object, the true object for all this depth of love which lies slumbering in our hearts, is God in Christ, the Christ that died for us.

Now, lastly, notice that terrible misdirection of these capacities is the sin and the misery of the world.

I will not say that such emotions, even when expended on creatures, are ever wasted. For however unworthy may be the objects on which they are lavished, the man himself is the better and the higher for having cherished them. The mother, when she forgets self in her child, though her love and self-forgetfulness and self-sacrifice may, in some respects, be called but an animal instinct, is elevated and ennobled by the exercise of them. The patriot and the thinker, the philanthropist, even—although I take him to be the lowest of the scale—the soldier who, in some cause which he thinks to be a good one, and not merely in the tigerish madness of the battlefield, throws away his life—are lifted in the scale of being by their self-abnegation.

And so I am not going to say that when men love each other passionately and deeply, and sacrifice themselves for one another, or for some cause or purpose affecting only temporal matters, the precious elixir of love is wasted. God forbid! But I do say that all these objects, sweet and gracious as some of them are, ennobling and elevating as some of them are, if they are taken apart from God, are insufficient to fill your hearts: and that if they are slipped in between you and God, as they often are, then they bring sin and sorrow.

There is nothing more tragic in this world than the misdirection of man's capacity for love and sacrifice.

It is like the old story in the Book of Daniel, which tells how the heathen monarch made a great feast, and when the wine began to inflame the guests, sent for the sacred vessels taken from the Temple of Jerusalem, that had been used for Jehovah's worship: and (as the narrative says, with a kind of shudder at the profanation), "They brought the golden vessels that were taken out of the temple of the House of God, which was at Jerusalem, and the king and his princes, his wives and his concubines, drank in them. They drank wine and praised the

VICTORY IN FAILURE

gods." So this heart of mine, which, as I said, has the Master's initials and His arms engraven upon it, in token that it is His cup, I too often fill with the poisonous and intoxicating draught of earthly pleasure and earthly affections; and as I drink it, the madness goes through my veins, and I praise gods of my own making instead of Him Whom alone I ought to love.

The heroism of the world should put to shame the cowardice and the selfishness of the Church. Contrast the depth of your affection for your household with the tepidity of your love for your Saviour. Contrast the willingness with which you sacrifice yourself for some dear one with the grudgingness with which you yield yourselves to Him. Contrast the rest and the sense of satisfaction in the presence of those you love, and your desolation when they are absent, with the indifference whether you have Christ beside you or not. And remember that the measure of your power of loving is the measure of your obligation to love your Lord; and that if you are all frost to Him and all fervor to them, then in a very solemn sense "a man's foes shall be they of his household." "He that loveth father or mother more than Me is not worthy of Me!"

I urge you to bring that power of uncalculating love and self-sacrificing affection and fasten it where it ought to fix—on Christ who died on the cross for you. Such a love will bring blessedness to you. Such a love will ennoble and dignify your whole nature, and make you a far greater and fairer man or woman than you otherwise ever could be.

Like some little bit of black carbon put into an electric current, my poor nature will flame into beauty and radiance when that spark touches it. So love Him and be at peace; give yourselves to Him and He will give you back yourselves, ennobled and transfigured by the surrender. Lay yourselves on His altar, and that altar will sanctify both the giver and the gift.

If you can take this rough Philistine soldier's words in their spirit, and in a higher sense, say, "Whether I live I live unto the Lord, or whether I die I die unto the Lord; living or dying, I am the Lord's," He will let you enlist in His army; and give you for your marching orders this command and this hope, "If any man serve Me let him follow Me; and where I am there shall also My servant be."

THIRST FOR GOD

O God, Thou art my God: early will I seek Thee: my soul thirsteth for Thee, my flesh longeth for Thee in a dry and thirsty land, where no water is; To see Thy power and Thy glory, so as I have seen Thee in the sanctuary. Because Thy lovingkindness is better than life, my lips shall praise Thee.

(PS. 63:1,2)

THIS PSALM CONTAINS very distinct traces of the circumstances under which it sprang up in the Psalmist's heart. He is an exile, in a dry and weary land; he is excluded from the sanctuary, he is followed by enemies that seek his life; he is a king. All these points confirm the accuracy of the ancient Jewish heading:—"A Psalm of David, when he was in the wilderness of Judah."

In that arid tract which stretches along the western shore of the Dead Sea, and thence northward, David was twice during his adventurous life—once during the Sauline persecution, once during Absalom's revolt. It cannot be the former of these times which is referred to here, because the Psalmist was not then a king; it must therefore be the latter.

That was the darkest hour of his life. His favorite and good-for-nothing son was seeking to grasp his scepter; his familiar friend in whom he trusted had lifted up the heel against him. He knew that his own sin had come back to roost with him; and so, with bleeding heart, with agonized conscience, with crushed spirit, he bowed himself, and meekly and penitently accepted the chastisement. Therefore it was sweetened to him; and this Psalm, with its passion of love and mystic rapture, is a closer union with God, as our sorrows may do for us; like some treasure washed to our feet by a stormy sea.

Let us read the Psalm over together and try to feel its force as the utterance of a soul seeking after and finding God. I think the key to its arrangement will be found in the threefold recurrence of an emphatic word. In the first verse I read, "My soul thirsteth for Thee;" in the fifth verse, "My soul shall be satisfied;" in the eighth verse, "My soul followeth hard after Thee." These three points, I think, are the turning points of the Psalm and they show us the soul longing; the longing soul satisfied; the satisfied soul still seeking. Let us take, then, these three thoughts, and look at them as the centerpoints of the respective portions of the Psalm to which they belong.

First, then, we have the soul longing for God.

Now, observe that this longing is not that of a man who has no possession of God. Rather is it the desire of a heart which is already in union with Him for a closer union; rather is it the tightening of the grasp with which the man already holds his Father in Heaven. All begins with the utterance of a personal appropriating faith. "Oh God! Thou art my God!" The beginning of all personal religion is when I am conscious of a personal relation with God; when I feel that He and I possess each other by a mutual love; when I put out my hand, and humbly but confidently claim my individual portion in the world-wide power and love. A Christian is he who says, "He loved *me*, and gave Himself for *me*." We must individualize, and appropriate as our very own, the promises and the grace that belong to the whole world. "O God! Thou art *my* God."

And then upon that there are built earnest seeking, expressed in the words "Early," that is to say, "earnestly," "will I seek Thee," and the intensest longing, breathing in the pathetic utterance, "My soul thirsteth for Thee: my flesh longeth for Thee in a dry and weary land where no water is." Notice the picturesque, poetic beauty of taking David's surroundings as the emblem of his

Thirst for God

feelings. Nature seems to reflect his mood. He looks out on the stony, monotonous, burnt-up, barren country about him; at the cracks in the soil gaping for the rain which comes not; and he sees the emblem of a heart yearning after God and not possessing Him. He and his men have been toiling, wearied, across "the burning marl," looking in all the torrent-beds of some drop of water to cool their parched throats, and finding none. And that seems to him like the search of a soul after a far-off God.

And then, notice what it is, or rather Whom it is that the Psalmist longs for. "My soul thirsts *for Thee.*" All souls do. We are all crying out for the living God, only the difference between us is that some of us know what it is that we want, and that some of us do not. Blessed are they who can say: "Thou art my God"; and who can add: "My soul thirsteth for *Thee,*" in Whom, and in Whom only, is the fountain at which we can all slake our thirst and be satisfied.

Notice the intensity of the desire. Think of the picture that rises from these graphic words. Here is the caravan toiling through the desert; men's lips are black with thirst, their parched tongues lolling from their mouths; a film comes over their glazing eyes, their steps totter, their heads throb. Far away yonder is a stunted tree which tells of water near it. How they plunge their faces into the black mud when they come to it, and with what a fierce passion they satisfy their cravings!

There is no such overmastering appetite as thirst. Is it the least like your desire after God? Can anybody say that these words of my text are an honest description of the ordinary experience of ordinary Christians? "My soul thirsteth for God"; cried this seeker after Him, and the longing seems to have affected even his bodily health. Is that or anything like it true, about you, brethren? What sort of Christians are we if it is not?

And notice *when* it was that this man thus longed. It was in the midst of his sorrow. Even then the thing that he wanted most was not restoration to Jerusalem, or the defeat of his enemies, but union with God. Oh! that is a test of faith, and one which very little of our faith could stand, that even when we are ringed about by calamities that seem to crush us, what we long for most is not the removal of the sorrow but the presence of our Father. Good men are driven to God by the stress of tempests, and ordinary and bad men are generally driven away from Him. What does your sorrow do for you, friend? Does it make you writhe in impatience, does it make you murmur sullenly against His imposition of it, or does it make you feel that now in the stress and agony there is nothing that you can grasp and hold to but Him, and Him alone? And so in the hour of darkness and need is your prayer, in its deepest meaning, not "Take away Thy heavy hand from me," but "Give me more of Thyself, that I may bear Thy hand, however heavy its pressure"?

Still looking at this first portion of our Psalm, of which that desire, intense and ardent, is the keynote, I notice that this longing, though it be struck out by sorrow, is not forced upon him for the first time by sorrow. The second verse of our Psalm might be more accurately rendered with the transposition of the two clauses, somewhat in this fashion: "So have I gazed upon Thee in the sanctuary, to see Thy power and Thy glory." That is to say, in like manner as in his sorrows and in the wilderness he is conscious of this desire after God, so does he remember that amidst the sanctities of the Tabernacle and the joyful services and sacrifices of

Thirst for God

its ritual worship he looked through the forms to Him that shone in them, and in them beheld His power and His glory. So the longing that springs in his heart is an old longing. He remembers past times when it has been with him, and his days of sorrow are not the first days in which he has been driven to say: "Come Thou and help me." He can remember glad, peaceful moments of communion, and these are homogeneous and of a piece with his religious contemplations in his hours of sorrow.

That life is but a poor, fragmentary one which seeks God by fits and starts; and that seeking after God is but a half-hearted and partial one which is only experienced in the moments of pain and grief. It is well to cry for Him in the wilderness, but it is not well that it should only be the wilderness in which we cry for Him. It is well when darkness and disaster teach us our need of Him; but it is not well when we require the darkness and the disaster to teach us our need.

And, on the other hand, that is but a poor, fragmentary life, and that religion is but a very incomplete and insincere one which is more productive of raptures in the sanctuary than of seeking after God in the wilderness. There are plenty of Christian people who have a great deal more consciousness of God's presence in the idle emotions of a church or a chapel than in the strenuous efforts of daily life. Both things separately are maimed and miserable; and both must be put together—the communion in the sanctuary and the communion in the wilderness; seeking after Him in the sanctities of worship, and seeking after Him in the prose of daily life—if ever the worship of the sanctuary or the prose of daily life are to be brightened with His presence.

Then, still further, this longing is animated by a profound consciousness that God is best. "Because Thy lovingkindness is better than life." Life is good mainly as the field upon which God's lovingkindness may be manifested and grasped. It is like the white sheet on which the beam of light is thrown, worth nothing in itself, worth everything as the medium for the manifestation of that lustrous light. It is like a painted window— only a poor bit of glass till the sunshine gleams behind it, and then it flashes up into rubies and purple and gold. Life is best when through life there filters or flashes on us the brightness of the lovingkindness of the Lord. And all real religion includes in it a calm, deliberate, fixed preference of God to life itself. Does your religion include that? Can you say, "It were wise and it were blessed to die, to get more of God into my soul"? If not, our longing, which is the very language of the Spirit in our hearts, has to be much intensified ere it reaches its fitting height.

And then, still further, this longing is accompanied with a firm resolve of continuance. "Thus will I bless Thee while I live." "Thus"—as I am doing now in the midst of my longing—" I will lift up my hands in Thy name." So much, then, for the first portion of the Psalm.

Now turn for a moment to the second portion, which is included in the next three verses, where we have the longing soul satisfied. "My soul shall be satisfied as with marrow and fatness."

Notice, now, how very beautiful that immediate turn in the Psalmist's feelings is. The fruition of God is contemporaneous with the desire after God. The one moment, "My soul thirsteth"; the next moment, "My soul is satisfied." As in the wilderness when the rain comes down, and in a couple of days what was baked earth is flowery meadow, and all the torrent-beds where the

Thirst for God

white stones glistened ghastly in the heat are foaming with rushing water, and fringed with budding willows; so in the instant in which a heart turns with true desire to God, in that instant does God draw near to it. The Arctic spring comes with one stride; to-day snow, to-morrow flowers. There is no time needed to work this telegraph; while we speak He hears; before we call He answers. We have to wait for many of His gifts, never for Himself. We have to wait sometimes when by our own faults we postpone the coming of the blessings that we have asked. If we are thinking more about Absalom and Ahitophel than about God; more about our sorrows and our troubles than about Himself; if we are busy with other things; if having asked we do not look up and expect; if we shut the doors of our hearts as soon as our prayer is offered, or languidly stroll away from the place of prayer ere the blessing has fluttered down upon our souls, of course we do not get it. But God is always waiting to bestow, and all that we need to do is to open the sluices and the great ocean flows in, or as much of it as our hearts can hold. "My soul thirsteth," is the experience of the one moment, and ere the clock has ticked again, "My soul shall be satisfied."

Then notice, the soul that possesses God is fed full. The emblem here, of course, is of a joyful feast, possibly of a sacrificial one; but the fact is that whoever has got a living hold of God and a little bit of God lovingly imbedded in his heart, has got as much as he needs. Between God and him there is such a correspondence as that He is the absolute and all-sufficient good. If I may so say, every hollow in my nature answers to a protuberance in His, and when you put the two together the little heart is filled by the great heart that has come

VICTORY IN FAILURE

in to it. We are at rest when we have God, and to long for Him is to insure the possession of an absolute and all-sufficient good.

We have here, still further, the satisfied soul breaking into the music of praise. "My mouth shall praise Thee with joyful lips when I remember Thee upon my bed, and meditate on Thee in the night-watches." There is a reference, no doubt, there, to the little camp in the wilderness, where David and his men, unguarded save by God, laid themselves down to sleep beneath the Syrian sky with all its stars, and where the leader, no doubt, often awoke in the night, with pricked-up ears listening for the sound of an approaching enemy. And even then into his heart there steals the thought of his great Protector; and as he says in another of the Psalms dating from this period, "I will lay me down in peace and sleep, because Thou makest me to dwell, though solitary, in safety." The heart that feeds upon God is secure, and breaks into songs in the night, and music of praise. That feast has always minstrels at it. The spontaneous utterance of a heart feeding on God is thankfulness and praise, which is as natural as smiles when we are glad, or as tears when we mourn.

And then, still further, this satisfaction leads on to a triumphant hope. "Because Thou hast been my help, therefore in the shadow of Thy wings will I rejoice." Such a past and such a present can only have one kind of future as their consequence—a future in which the seeking soul nestling beneath the great outstretched wings shall crowd close to the Father's heart, and be guarded by His love. If we hold fellowship with Him He protects us. As another Psalm says, using a similar metaphor: "He that dwelleth in the secret place of the Most High shall abide under the shadow of the Almighty." Communion

Thirst for God

with God means protection by God.

The past of the seeking soul is the certain pledge of its future. The uncertainties of the dim to-morrow, in so far as earth is concerned, are so many that we can never say, "To-morrow shall be as this day." And in regard of all other sources of blessing, the dearest and the purest, we have all to feel, with sinking, sickening hearts, that the longer we have had them the nearer comes the day of their certain loss. But about Him we can say, "Because Thou *hast* been my Helper, therefore in the shadow of Thy wings *will* I rejoice." And in union with Him we can look out over all the dim sea that stretches before us, and though we know not what storms may vex the surface, or whither its currents may carry us, we can say, "Thou wilt be with Me, and in Thee I shall have peace."

Lastly, the final section of this Psalm gives us the satisfied soul still seeking after God. "My soul followeth hard after Thee, Thy right hand upholdeth me."

The word translated *followeth* here literally means *to cleave or to cling*. And there is a beautiful double idea of a twofold relationship expressed in that somewhat incongruous form of speech, "cleave after Thee," the former word giving the idea of union and possession, the latter suggesting the other idea of search and pursuit. So that the two main currents of thought in the Psalm are repeated in that little phrase: and we are back again—though with a wonderful difference—to the ground tone of the first section. There the soul thirsteth; here "the soul cleaveth after"—both expressive of pursuit, but the latter, as consequent upon the satisfaction which followed upon the thirst, speaks of a profounder possession and of a less painful sense of want.

"My soul cleaveth after God." That is to say, inasmuch as He is infinite, and this nature of mine capable of indefinite expansion, each new possession of Him which follows upon an enlarged desire will open the elastic walls of my heart so that they shall enclose a wider space and be capable of holding more of God, and therefore I shall possess more. Desire expands the heart; possession expands the heart. More of God comes when we can hold more of Him, and the end of all fruition is the renewed desire after further fruition.

This world's gifts cloy and never satisfy; God satisfies and never cloys. And we have, and we shall have, if we are His children, the double delight of a continued fruition, and a continued desire. So we shall ascend, if I may so say, in ever higher and higher spirals, which will rise further and draw in more closely towards the unreached and unattainable Throne of the blessed Himself, "My soul thirsteth"; "my soul is satisfied"; "my satisfied soul still longs and follows."

And then there is also very beautifully here, the cooperation, and reciprocal action of the seeking soul and of the sustaining God. "My soul followeth hard after Thee; Thy right hand upholdeth me." We hold and we are held. We hold because we are held, and we are held while we hold. We follow, and yet He is with us; we long, and yet we possess; we pursue, and yet in the very act of pursuit we are upheld by His hand. We should not follow unless He held us up. He will not hold us up unless we follow. All controversies of grace and freewill are reconciled and lulled to sleep in these great words.

And now I can but lightly touch upon the last portion of the Psalm, which describes one consequence of pressing after God. The soul thus cleaving and following is gifted with a prophetic certainty. "Those that seek my soul are destined for destruction" (so is the probable rendering); "they shall go into the lower parts of the earth"—swallowed up like Korah and his rebellious company. "They shall each be given up to the power of the sword" (as the words might be rendered); "they shall be a portion for foxes" (or *jackals*, as the word means). Their unburied bodies shall lie in the wilderness, and the jackals shall tear and devour them. David regarded his enemies as God's enemies. David's point of view permitted him to exult with a stern but not unrighteous joy in their destruction. But these words are not prayer nor imprecation, but prophecy and the insight of a soul conscious of union with God, and therefore assured that everything which stands in the way of its possession of God Whom it loves is destined for annihilation.

And, disengaging the words from the mere husk and shell of Old Testament experience, all of us, if we cleave to God, may have this confidence, that nothing can hinder our fellowship with God; and that whatsoever stands in the way of our closer union with Him shall be swept out of the way. David's certainty of the destruction of his foes is the same triumphant assurance, on a lower spiritual level, as Paul's trumpet-blast of victory. "Who shall separate us from the love of God? Shall tribulation, or distress, or persecution, or famine, or nakedness, or peril, or sword?" "Nay, in all these things,"—and over all these things—"we are more than conquerors through Him that loved us."

There is the other side of this prophetic certainty here. "The king shall rejoice in God; every one that sweareth by Him shall glory." He and his faithful followers shall realize a divine deliverance, which shall be the subject of their praise; and the adversary's lips shall be sealed with silence, their vindication shall stick in their throat, and they shall be dumb before the judgment of Almighty God. That confidence too may stand as a symbol of the certainty of hope which refreshes the soul which seeks and possesses God, even in the wilderness and while compassed with sorrows and fears. We, too, may find in our present union with God a prophecy fixed and firm as the pillars of His throne, of our future kingly dignity, and rapturous joy in Him. It is reserved not for us only but for all whose lips confessed Him on earth and shall therefore be opened to lift up before Him triumphant praise, which shall drown the discords of opposing voices, and no more be broken by sobs or weeping.

We are all thirsty. Do you know what it is that makes you restless? Do you know Who it is that you need? Listen to Him that says: "If any man thirst let him come to Me and drink." Choose whether you will be tortured with mad and aimless cravings, and perish in a dry land; or whether you will come to the Fountain of Life in Christ your Saviour, and slake your thirst at God Himself.

YOUR INHERITANCE IS WAITING

Kept by the power of God, through faith, unto salvation.
(1 PETER 1:5)

THERE IS A PICTURE HERE which is somewhat obscured in our Authorized Version by the use of the expression "kept." What that picture is will be plain to you if I note that it is the same word which the Apostle Paul uses when he is talking about the Governor under King Aretas who guarded the city of Damascus. And it is the same word which the same apostle employs, with the same metaphorical reference as here, when he talks about the peace of God guarding or garrisoning men's hearts and minds in Christ Jesus. That is to say, we are to think of some little undefended village which is made safe because a strong force is thrown into it; and then, though it be a city broken down, without walls, it is impregnable. Peter thinks that every Christian has enemies that he cannot beat back alone; and he thinks that every Christian man *may* have round him a ring of defense against which all enemies will break and throw themselves away like impotent waves against a breakwater. That is the first point to notice in the words. There is another, very familiar to you all; and I am not going to say anything this morning which is not familiar to us. Notice the close connection between the words of my text and the immediately preceding words, "an inheritance reserved in heaven for you who are kept," guarded, that is to say. The one Divine Power is working on both sides of the curtain, preserving the inheritance for the heirs, preserving the heirs for the inheritance. It will not fail them, they will not miss it. And so the earthward aspect of this double guarding by the power of God is our theme this morning, and I am going to be most childishly simple. By, through, unto. There are three aspects under which Peter describes the guarding which is the prerogative of every Christian. He deals with its efficient causal origin by the power of God, he deals with its condition or means, through faith; he deals with its ultimate end, unto salvation. If we turn the thing about and begin at the end we shall be going logically.

First, I want you to consider what the guarding is for. Unto salvation! It was a new word and a new thought to Peter's readers, and just because it was new and strange they could not get themselves right into it, and did not understand the sweep and the depth of it. You and I do not understand the sweep and the depth of it for precisely the opposite reason. You all think you know all about it. You have heard it until you are weary, and like a sixpenny piece by much attrition, the lines and the letterings are faded. But I want to try to bring back some of the morning freshness to that great thought that rose upon a darkened world in the early days of Christianity. A bit of seaweed, as long as it is in the ocean, has the wavelets expanding its delicate fronds, and brightening its sober color. But lift it out, and it is dry and dim. And you have got to take these familiar, commonplace Christian ideas and plunge them into an ocean of devout meditation, so to speak, and they will open out into all their pristine beauty, and be felt in all their power. Now, what the New Testament means by this dry, technical, theological word that we are all tired of, what the New Testament means by it is, first of all, making safe, and then making well. It implies a previous condition under a double aspect; peril threatening the life, disease culminating in death. And that is the diagnosis of humanity—very unfashionable to-day—which underlies the Christian conception of salvation; that men and women are in awful peril, and that men and women are drawing nigh to the gates of death. And this salvation comes in to dissipate the danger and to root out the disease. Do you know anything about that, about the view of humanity and that view of yourselves, which makes the message that you are safe and the message that you are healed, a gospel? And then there is another thing. On the one hand, and negatively, this notion of salvation, in the Christian fullness and depth of the idea, means the deliverance from all sorts of evils, whether of sin or of sorrow; and on the other hand, and positively, it means the investing with all sorts of good, and whether moral or material.

And that completeness of making safe and making whole is not all that lies in the word. You think of salvation mainly as being barring the gates of hell, enabling you to dodge the consequences of your sins. No, that is not the New Testament notion. We must be delivered from the danger, also invested with all the good. And if you notice the apostle, writing in my text, means by this salvation, which is the ultimate end of the Divine dealings; precisely the same thing which he meant a breath before his inheritance; he meant the same thing. And what was that? Getting God for my own; not only on my side, but into my spirit. That is salvation, and that is the inheritance, and nobody understands the magnificent possibilities that lie in the initial Christian salvation unless far beyond any escape from penal consequences, he had risen to the conception that the essence of salvation is the possession of God. You may call that mysticism if you like. If your Christianity has not that element of mysticism in it, it is shallow, if it is real. But notice still further that in our text the apostle is speaking about this great inheritance of salvation as a thing in the future. That, of course, I do not mean to elaborate. But I do wish to draw your attention to the fact that a verse or two afterwards he talks about it as a thing presently possessed, and contemporaneous with, because always consequent upon, the act of faith. He says, "Believing, ye rejoice, receiving the end of your faith, *even* the salvation of your souls." So there is a salvation away ahead, yonder to which all the operations of the Divine providence and of the Divine grace are conducting men. Ah! but the end of the rope is in my hand here, however far off may be the balloon that is attached to it at the other; and the germ of that perfection in the heavens must be here, to-day, in the experiences of earth. There is nothing else that will correspond to the facts of the Christian life here below, except that full deliverance from all evil, and that entire investiture with all the good in God that a human soul capable of Divine expression can gather unto itself; there is nothing else that will correspond to the facts of the Christian life here except that. You look at a row of houses put up in some growing suburb like this, and you will find often that at the end of the row, so far as it has gone already, there are protruding bricks. What do they mean? They mean that there is another house coming. And the facts of the Christian life here on earth, its greatness and its smallness, its failures and its successes, its moments of elevation, and its moments of depression, all proclaim with one voice: "This is not the adequate manifestation of the Power that has produced it; that which has been able to do so much and no more must be able to do infinitely more when it gets fair play." The new moon, with her ragged edge, even in its imperfection, is beautiful; it prophesies the placid completeness of the silver roundness by every inequality

Your Inheritance Is Waiting

on the line of present vision. And the perfect salvation is the only thing that will correspond to the lives of Christian men here. Yes, it is the only thing that will correspond to the energies that have been brought into play in order to produce it. That entire deliverance from all evil, that all-swathing investiture with all good, is the end for which Jesus Christ came and lived and died, and He is not going to be balked of the travail of His soul, and nothing less than that complete gift to all that believe on Him would be an adequate motive for Him to suffer, and an adequate reward for Him who has suffered. Such complete salvation is the end of all God's discipline of us here, and nothing else and nothing less would be the adequate explanation of His providence to us upon earth. God is not going to be guilty of an unDivine disproportion of means to end. And the means that He has set in operation, the incarnation and sacrifice of Jesus Christ, the Father of His providences, and the deep, unfathomable wisdom of His dealings with us, His guidance and His guardianship, will not be in vain, but they will lead on to the conditions that my text deals with presently, lead unto salvation.

What we are guarded *for* leads next to what we are guarded *by*. By the power of God. Now, I incline to believe that there is another picture suggested there, and if you will pardon me—I know people do not like expository preaching—I would like to show cause for my belief. "Kept by the power of God." Well, now, to read that quite literally would be to say kept *in* the power of God. And though the *by* is a perfectly legitimate explanation of the apostle's meaning, don't you see how much more beauty and picturesque force is given if we take the other notion, and say kept, guarded, *in* the power, as if it was round about us, and we were deposited

VICTORY IN FAILURE

there in the middle of it? "The name of the Lord is a strong tower; the righteous runneth into it, and is safe. He that dwelleth in the secret place of the Most High"—and that does not mean the secret place that belongs to the Most High, but the secret place that the Most High constitutes—"He that dwelleth in the secret place of the Most High shall abide under the shadow"—of course he will if he is close in; he is sure to be in the shadow of the wall that rises above him. And so, as another old Psalm has it, taking substantially the same metaphor as in my text, "The angel of the Lord"—not the angels—"the angel of the Lord encampeth round about them that fear Him." "Kept in the power." When an army is marching through an enemy's country, they put the women and children and the invalids in the middle, and then they are safe. And that is where you and I will be safe, inserted into God, if I may venture upon such a phrase. And that is not too strong a phrase; it is not half as strong as the Master's "Abide *in* Me and I *in* you, for apart from Me ye"—not merely can do, but—"ye are nothing." Brethren in Christ, I was going to be very heterodox, and say even more than Christ for us is the word for the growing Christian. It is well, and we have all to begin with looking upon the Saviour as the sacrifice for your sins, but that is introductory to our being able to comprehend Him as the indwelling power of our lives, and as the refuge in whom we have to abide. So although it is of course true that the power of God is the instrument whereby we are kept, it is also true that the means whereby that power of God exercises its guarding influence is by bringing us within itself and keeping itself around us. For let us never forget that the power of God guards the Christian by means of the imparted Spirit of God, and only in the degree in which we receive into ourselves that Divine infuence will it avail to preserve us from the evils that are without. The communication for us to keep ourselves is the means by which the power of God keeps us. And whilst for all strength to guard ourselves we must ever be looking to Him and drawing it from Him, that is not all that we have to do, but rather we have to remember the word "Keep yourselves in the love of God," as well as to fall back upon the blessed words that are here, "Guarded by the Power of God."

And, now, lastly, we have considered what we are guarded for, and what we are guarded by. Now we will consider what we are guarded through. Through faith. There you come to another wonderful sixpence, another word that has been so mauled about that people have no definite idea attached to it. I sometimes wish we could give it a dispensation from appearing in public ministrations for twenty years, and get something to answer as well for it. And there is a word that does answer for it. Suppose instead of the old theological conception "kept by the power of God through faith," we simply said, "Kept by the power of God through trust"? Does not that sound much truer, less abstract? And it is the exact rendering of the New Testament idea. And so people say it is a very immoral thing, this Christian teaching, that a man is saved by faith. They say, "Man is not responsible for his belief, and if he were, an intellectual belief is by no means the thing that ought to be recompensed by salvation." Well, if salvation were a thing that could be handed out over a counter to anybody, irrespective altogether of what that was, if it could be given as a medal is given to a child, then the criticism might have some force. Or, if the New Testament teaching were that salvation was the result of intellectual belief, then the criticism would have a great deal of force. But neither of the two things are true. Faith is not belief, if by belief you mean saying "Yes; I assent and consent to these Thirty-nine Articles or thirty-nine thousand." But faith is an act of the whole moral nature of a man, and there is *Will* in it, which there never ought to be in acts of belief. You ought not to believe intellectually as you choose; you must exercise faith by choosing, and thereby draw a distinction, which no one can obliterate or get over, between the mere acceptance of a creed and the act of trust in which the will and the affections are implicated quite as much as the intellect.

There is another thing to be said, and that is that faith, which is the condition of salvation and of the guarding with a view to salvation, has for its object not a doctrine, but a Person. You *believe* doctrines, you *trust* people. And you may believe Jesus Christ to all eternity, and yet it will bring you no salvation; but if you believe *on* Him, then you will rejoice with joy unspeakable.

And there is another thing to be said, and that is, that the faith which is the condition of salvation is not only as an act of the will, trust, and reposing upon a person and grappling him to one's heart, but that also there must be in it an inseparable element of self-abandonment and distrust. You put a seed into your little gardens in this spring weather, and after a little while one little radicle strikes downwards, and another little outgrowth comes upwards. The one is the root, the other is the stem of the future plant, but they both come out of that seed. Faith is the upward strike, self-distrust is the downward one. And no man ever gets to Jesus Christ until he has been very near despair and has looked it in the eyeballs. And so the thing which is the condition of salvation is trust, trust in a person, trust accompanied with absolute self-distrust and abandonment. That is the condition, and there is nothing arbitrary about that being a condition. If God could have saved the world without faith He would have done it, never fear. And it is not by His appointment, but by the varying necessities of the case that salvation comes through faith and through nothing besides. Is it arbitrary that if you put a shutter upon that window no sunlight will come in? Is it arbitrary that if you do not take your medicine you will not be cured? Is it arbitrary that if you do not pull the trigger the pistol will not go off? No more is it arbitrary that without faith no man shall see salvation. Brethren, when Jesus Christ was here upon earth we read that He could there do no mighty works because of their unbelief. Ah! Omnipotence may be hampered and the Almighty arm may not have elbow-room to do its work by our unbelief. And I am sure that in a congregation like this there are some people who have thus thwarted and hampered the Omnipotent power and utilized the all-loving purpose. If we will, as this man Peter did, cry, "Lord, save me, I perish," the hand will come out. Would it have been arbitrary if Peter had been drowned if he had not put out his hand to be grasped? And that is all you and I have got to do; but we have got to do it. Salvation here and hereafter is God's gift. It cannot be given without faith; it is given to every man that exercises faith.

VICTORY OVER COLDNESS

These things saith he that hath the seven spirits of God and the seven stars
(REV. 3:1)

IT HAD NO PERSECUTIONS like the faithful band at Smyrna. Why should it? It had not life enough to be obnoxious! What was there in such a church as that to provoke any antagonism? It exactly suited the world's purpose, and was, in fact, only a bit of the world under another name. A dead Church is on the best possible terms with a dead world. This Church at Sardis had no heresies, it had not life enough in it to grow them.

When the frost binds the ground, weeds and flowers alike cease to be put forth. So the Church at Sardis had no heretics because nobody in it cared enough about the principles of Christianity to think earnestly about them. And it had no immoralities either—most respectable, and standing high in all the common moralities of life! And yet one Eye looked at it and said, "Thou hast a name that thou livest, and are dead." About how many of our churches and of the individual Christians who take up the profession of Christ and connect themselves with ecclesiastical arrangements with such light hearts, may the same be said!

If we want to understand what the deadness predicated of this Sardian church was, let us remember that the words are Christ's own, and that life is the condition of union with Jesus Christ, and death is the grim alternative that waits upon separation from Him. That church had lost the tenacity of its hold and the intimacy of its union with Jesus Christ; it had no clear operative conception of Him, His will, His truth, His love; its love had been clogged and alienated from Him, and so had become flaccid and feeble; its communion with Him had been languid, dull, interrupted, and therefore the separation had wrought its necessary effects, and down, *down*, DOWN, ever deeper down into the depth and darkness of the cold grave went a body of people that had once been vitalized by the touch of Him, and by the loss of His touch had sunk. Wherever a Christian individual or a Christian community loses the simplicity and tenacity of its grip on Jesus Christ, there the life ebbs out of it, and "thou hast a name that thou livest, and art dead."

Now note that such a condition is not final and irreversible. The very fact that the letter came to that community indicates that it was possible to restore and revive. They were not so utterly dead as moribund, and so in another part of the letter we read about things which remain and are ready to die, and about works which were done but were not perfect or fulfilled. Effects last after causes cease; institutions live when all the reality is out of them. Habit, use and wont, forms, ceremonies, keep up the appearance of vitality when the reality is almost gone; and there is many a man who is a nominal adherent of some cause or creed, be it religious or otherwise, with no convictions at the back of his nominal profession. There are creatures of a low organization where you can get muscular contractions after life is extinct; there is such a thing as a train running for a quarter of a mile when the steam is shut off and it is on a dead level; you will find gardens round many a deserted, roofless house in the country where the weeds have not killed all the roses, and a vagrant flower or two still remains to testify the culture that was.

So in thousands of our communities there is enough left of the living, lingering effect of the primitive impulse

Victory over Coldness

to keep up a ghastly mockery of life which would be far better if it knew itself to be what it is—dead! And that brings me to say again that such a condition may be absolutely concealed from every eye but the Eye that is as a flame of fire. "Thou hast a name that thou livest." That congregation has a high reputation in its denomination for activity and liberality and Christian graces; that church stands out as being vigorous, and wholesome, and healthy; that man is thought of as being distinctly a Christian man, and a Christian man of the true sort: and all the while He is saying, "a name, a name that thou livest." A great many of our communities I am afraid are living on the past. Those who are resting on traditions and former victories had better be carried out of the way as soon as possible!

It is not only to outside observers that use and wont and the repetition of forms and ceremonies masks the ebbing out of the spiritual life. Nobody would be more astonished at this verdict of the faithful witness than were the people at Sardis that were affected by it. Cannot you hear them when the letter was read to them? Cannot you hear them anticipating the other cry, "Lord! Lord! have we not prophesied in Thy name?" "Are we not Thine?" Unconsciousness is the surest sign of spiritual decline. I suppose a man paralyzed has no sense in his limbs, and might put his feet into a tub of scalding water and take the flesh off the bones and never know it. Frostbitten limbs are perfectly comfortable: it is the waking that is the pain. When a man can say, "I am half asleep," he is more than half awake. The less a professing Christian man is conscious of declension the more likely he is to be affected by it. These people in Sardis had gone so far down that they could not turn their heads up to see how high they had once been—"Thou hast forgotten," says the letter, "from whence thou hast fallen," and the first thing that dies out of moribund Christians is the ideal of a higher life, and so they become contented and ignorant of their true condition. Like the hero of the Old Testament Book with his locks cropped, they go out as of old to exercise themselves, and they wist not that their strength has departed from them till they try a death-grapple with the Philistines, and then they find it out fast enough.

What is it that has in the course of ages worn into the indistinctness the sharp-cut granite features of the Sphinx that looks out over the Egyptian desert? The perpetual attrition of microscopic grains of sand blown against it by the vagrant winds! And so the multitudinous trivialities of life, coming in contact with the image of Jesus Christ in our hearts, will efface its fair features and leave but a dim outline. Therefore we ought to give the more earnest heed to the things that we have heard, and to the person that we have heard saying the things, lest at any time we should be drifted past him and them.

Now, in the second place, look with me at the vision which such a Church needs—"He that hath the seven spirits of God and the seven stars." The seven spirits have already been spoken of in the previous chapter; they are again noticed in subsequent parts of the letter under the two emblems of the seven lamps which are before the throne of God, and the seven eyes which go forth into all the earth. That means, of course, illumination and omniscience, but it means a great deal more than that; it is a distinct reference to the personal spirit of God conceived of in the manifoldness of His operations rather than in the unity of His Personality. And these emblems declare that like the swift flash of the lamp and the swift glance of the eye that rolls over all the visible

Victory over Coldness

that spirit comes permeating, enlightening, illuminating, vivifying, discerning, and strengthening all of us if we yield ourselves to it. There is the antidote for a dead Church, a living spirit in the sevenfold perfectness of His operations. He is the spirit of consolation, of adoption, of supplication, of holiness and wisdom, of power and of love, and of a sound mind, and into all our deadness there will come the life-breath which shall surely quicken it all.

Here, and here only, as it seems to me, is the hope of a dead Church, and here is the explanation of that which is unique in the history of Christianity as compared with all other religions, its power of self-recuperation, and when it is apparently nearest extinction, the marvelous, the miraculous way in which it flames up again because the spirit of the Lord is poured forth. It brings into prominence not so much the existence and the operations of that Divine spirit who vitalizes the Church as the continual energy and activity of the ascended Christ in bestowing that spirit. He hath the seven spirits as He has all other attributes; Himself in His earthly life being filled with its fulness, and it abiding with Him for ever, He has it to impart. There is the differentia of Christianity, and of the relation of its Founder to His followers, separating Him and them from all disciples of other schools and followers of other teachers. Other teachers—what can they do? They can impart a system, they can train a little group of dwindled imitators, who generally imitate their weaknesses, and think they are imitating their strength, but to give the spirit that animated the originator is exactly what none of them can do. And Elijah's answer to Elisha remains as the limit of all that other religious reformers and originators are able to perform: "I do not know whether you can get a portion of my spirit or not; if you do it is not I that gives it you." But Jesus Christ comes and says to us all, "If I depart I will send Him unto you," and that is a promise which the average Christian of this day by no means treats as the literal and all-important thing that it really is.

Look to the Christ that died on His cross having wrought the redemption of the whole world, and do not let that great fundamental truth obscure the truth of the Christ which is in us by His spirit to make us partakers of the fulness of His own life and the beginnings of His own holiness. You are to testify to that continuous activity of the Lord Jesus Christ in the bestowing of His Spirit all through the ages upon His Church. We have to look back to the cross, we have to feel that our salvation is not all secured by that past fact considered as a past fact, but needs further the continuous energy of the living Christ, and the continuous coming of the life-giving Spirit.

There are great diversities of opinion as to what exactly is meant by the seven stars. Some people say guardian angels, though it seems a strange mixing of the earthly and the heavenly to send letters to guardian angels. Some people say "ideal representatives." That may be, and, if so, He that hath the seven spirits and the seven stars suggests, if I might make a picture out of it, how He stands with the empty vessels in one hand and the golden oil vessel in the other, in order to replenish and to fill their emptiness. But there is a third explanation of the angel of the Church and that is that he was the bishop of the Church. And if so, don't you see how strikingly and beautifully there comes this thought—"He that hath the seven spirits and the seven stars"? One way by which that Spirit of God is shed abroad upon His

Victory over Coldness

moribund Church is by raising up men in it filled with the Spirit, and whose intense vitality communicates life to that which is almost dead.

Life is waiting to be bestowed upon us! Let this vision hearten us when we are conscious of our deadness; let it make us ask ourselves why it is that we have not more life. When the water does not come into your house in the winter-time, why is it? Because there is a plug of ice in the pipe; and that is why there is so little of the Water of Life in our experience, because we have stopped the connecting medium with our cold. There are three things needed for life—food, air, exercise. For food you have got Christ the Bread—see that you feed on Him; for air you have got the respiration of prayer—see that you draw the life-breath into your veins thereby; for exercise you have got Christian work, and daily living in the shops, or studies, or kitchens, or nurseries, or wherever God's Providence sets you—see that you bring your Christianity into operation, and then it will flourish. There are a great many of our professing brethren, the verdict over whose dead religion ought to be what is sometimes returned by a coroner's jury. *"Found dead in bed."*

When Abraham had made his escapade down into Egypt, and came back again very much ashamed of himself, he began his new career in the land by going to the place where he was at first. And that is where you and I must go, for our spiritual life can only be continued by that which at first evoked and communicated it—that is, by clinging to the cross of Christ, and putting ourselves into His hands.

So let us go and grasp His dear hand, and nothing is more unlikely than that we shall fail to feel the afflatus of

VICTORY IN FAILURE

His breath upon us as of old when He said, "Receive ye the Holy Ghost," because He lives, and in some measure as He lives, and as long as He lives, we shall live also, and the law of the spirit of life in Jesus Christ shall make us free from the law of sin and death!

FOOTSTEPS TO FORGIVENESS

Wash me thoroughly from mine iniquity, and cleanse me from my sin.
For I acknowledge my transgressions: and my sin is ever before me.

(PS. 51:2,3)

ADVERSITY HAD TAUGHT David self-restraint, had braced his soul, had driven him to grasp firmly the hand of God. And prosperity had seemed for nearly twenty years but to perfect the lessons. Gratitude had followed deliverance, and the sunshine after the rain had brought out the fragrance of devotion and the blossoms of glad songs. A good man, and still more a man of David's age at the date of his great crime, seldom falls so low, unless there has been previous, perhaps unconscious, relaxation of the girded loins, and negligence of the untrimmed lamp. The sensitive nature of the psalmist was indeed not unlikely to yield to the sudden force of such a temptation as conquered him, but we can scarcely conceive of its having done so without a previous decay of his religious life, hidden most likely from himself. And the source of the decay may probably be found in self-indulgence, fostered by ease, and by long years of command. The actual fall into sin seems to have been begun by slothful abdication of his functions as captain of Israel.

It is perhaps not without bitter emphasis that the narrative introduces it by telling us that, "at the time when kings go forth to battle," David contented himself with sending his troops against Ammon, and "tarried still at Jerusalem." At all events, the story brings into sharp contrast the levy *en masse*, encamped round Rabbath, and their natural head, who had once been so ready to take his share of blows and privations, loitering behind, taking his quiet siesta in the hot hours after noon, as if there had been no soldiers of his sweltering in their armour, and rising from his bed to stroll on his palace roof, and peer into the household privacies below, as if his heart had no interest in the grim tussle going on behind the hills that he could almost see from his height, as they grew purple in the evening twilight. He has fallen to the level of an Eastern despot, and has lost his sense of the responsibilities of his office. Such loosening of the tension of his moral nature as is indicated in his absence from the field, during what was evidently a very severe as well as a long struggle, prepared the way for the dismal headlong plunge into sin.

The story is told in all its hideousness, without palliation or reserve, without comment or heightening, in that stern judicial fashion so characteristic of the Bible records of its greatest characters. Every step is narrated without a trace of softening, and without a word of emotion. Not a single ugly detail is spared. The portraiture is as vivid as ever. Bathsheba's willing complicity, her punctilious observance of ceremonial propriety while she is trampling under foot her holiest obligations; the fatal necessity which drags sin after sin, and summons up murder to hide, if it be possible, the foul form of adultery; the stinging rebuke in the conduct of Uriah, who, Hittite as he was, has a more chivalrous, not to say devout, shrinking from personal ease while his comrades and the ark are in the field, than the king has; the mean treason, the degradation implied in getting into Joab's power; the cynical plainness of the murderous letter, in which a hardened conscience names his purposed evil by its true name; the contemptuous measure of his master which Joab takes in his message, the king's indifference to the loss of his men so long as Uriah is out of the way; the solemn platitudes with which he pretends to console his tool for the check of his troops; and the hideous haste with which, after her scrupulous "mourning" for one week, Bathsheba threw herself again into David's arms—all these particulars, and every particular an aggravation, stand out for ever, as men's most hidden evil will one day do, in the clear, unpitying, unmistakable light of the Divine record. What a story it is!

This saint of nearly fifty years of age, bound to God by ties which he rapturously felt and acknowledged, whose words have been the very breath of devotion for every devout heart, forgets his longings after righteousness, flings away the joys of Divine communion, darkens his soul, ends his prosperity, brings down upon his head for all his remaining years a cataract of calamities, and makes his name and his religion a target for the barbed sarcasms of each succeeding generation of scoffers. "All the fences and their whole array," which God's mercies and his own past had reared, "one cunning sin sweeps quite away." Every obligation of his office, as every grace of his character, is trodden under foot by the wild beast roused in his breast. As man, as king, as soldier, he is found wanting. Lust and treason, and craft and murder, are goodly companions for him who had said, "I will walk within my house with a perfect heart. I will set no wicked thing before mine eyes." Why should we dwell on the wretched story? Because it teaches us, as no other page in the history of God's church does, how the alchemy of Divine love can extract sweet perfumes of penitence and praise out of the filth of sin; and therefore, though we turn with loathing from David's sin, we have to bless God for the record of it, and for the lessons of hope that come from David's pardon.

To many a sin-tortured soul since then, the two psalms (51 and 32) all blotted with tears, in which he has

VICTORY IN FAILURE

sobbed out his penitence, have been as footsteps in a great and terrible wilderness. Of these two psalms, the fifty-first is evidently earlier than the thirty-second. In the former we see the fallen man struggling up out of the "horrible pit and miry clay"; in the latter he stands upon the rock, with a new song in his mouth, even the blessedness of him "whose sin is covered." It appears also that both must be dated after the sharp thrust of God's lancet which Nathan drove into his conscience, and the healing balsam of God's assurance of forgiveness which Nathan laid upon his heart. The passionate cries of the psalm are the echo of the Divine promise—the effort of his faith to grasp and keep the merciful gift of pardon. The consciousness of forgiveness is the basis of the prayer for forgiveness.

Somewhere about a year passed between the crime and the message of Nathan. And what sort of a year it was the psalms tell us. The coarse satisfactions of his sin could not long content him, as they might have done a lower type of man. Nobody buys a little passing pleasure in evil at so dear a rate, or keeps it for so short a time as a good man. He cannot make himself as others. "That which cometh into your mind shall not be at all, in that ye say, We will be as the families of the nations, which serve wood and stone." Old habits quickly reassert their force, conscience soon lifts again its solemn voice; and while worse men are enjoying the strong-flavoured meats on sin's table, the servant of God, who has been seduced to prefer them for a moment to the "light bread" from heaven, tastes them already bitter in his mouth. He may be far from true repentance, but he will very soon know remorse. Months may pass before he can feel again the calm joys of God, but disgust with himself and with his sin will quickly fill his soul. No more vivid picture of such a state has ever been drawn, than is found in the psalms of this period. They tell of sullen "silence"; dust had settled on the strings of his harp, as on helmet and sword. He will not speak to God of his sin, and there is nothing else that he can speak of. They tell of his "roaring all the day long"—the groan of anguish forced from his yet unsoftened spirit. Day and night God's heavy hand weighed him down; the consciousness of that power, whose gentleness had once holden him up, crushed, but did not melt him. Like some heated iron, its heaviness scorched as well as bruised, and his moisture—all the dew and freshness of his life—was dried up at its touch and turned into dusty, cracking drought, that chaps the hard earth, and shrinks the streamlets, and burns to brown powder the tender herbage (Ps. 32). Body and mind seem both to be included in this wonderful description, in which obstinate dumbness, constant torture, dread of God, and not one softening drop of penitence fill the dry and dusty heart, while "bones waxing old," or, as the word might be rendered, "rotting," sleepless nights, and perhaps the burning heat of disease, are hinted at as the accompaniments of the soul-agony. It is possible that similar allusions to actual bodily illness are to be found in another psalm, probably referring to the same period, and presenting striking parallelisms of expression (Ps. 6), "Have mercy upon me, Jehovah, for I languish (fade away); heal me, for my bones are affrighted. My soul is also sore vexed. I am weary with my groaning; every night make I my bed to swim. I water my couch with my tears." The similar phrase, too, in psalm fifty-one, "The bones which Thou hast broken," may have a similar application. Thus, sick in body and soul, he dragged through a weary year—ashamed of his guilty dalliance, wretched in his self-accusation, afraid of God, and skulking in the recesses of his palace from the sight of his people. A goodly price he had sold integrity for. The bread had been sweet for a moment, but how quickly his "mouth is filled with gravel" (Proverbs 20:17). David learned, what we all learn (and the holier a man is, the more speedily and sharply does the lesson follow on the heels of his sin), that every transgression is a blunder, that we never get the satisfaction which we expect from any sin, or if we do, we get something with it which spoils it all. A nauseous drug is added to the exciting, intoxicating drink which temptation offers, and though its flavor is at first disguised by the pleasanter taste of the sin, its bitterness is persistent though slow, and clings to the palate long after that has faded utterly.

Into this dreary life Nathan's message comes with merciful rebuke. The prompt severity of David's judgment against the selfish sinner of the inimitable apologue may be a subtle indication of his troubled conscience, which fancies some atonement for his own sin in stern repression of that of others; for consciousness of evil may sometimes sting into harshness as well as soften to lenity, and sinful man is a sterner judge than the righteous God. The answer of Nathan is a perfect example of the Divine way of convincing of sin. There is first a plain charge pressed home on the individual conscience, "Thou art the man." Then follows, not reproach nor further deepening of the blackness of the deed, but a tender enumeration of God's great benefits, whereon is built a solemn question, "Wherefore hast thou despised the commandment of the Lord, to do evil in His sight?" The contemplation of God's faithful love, and of the all-sufficient gifts which it bestows, makes every transgression irrational as well as ungrateful, and turns remorse, which consumes like the hot wind of the wilderness, into tearful

"The Lord has also put away thy sin"

repentance which refreshes the soul. When God has been seen loving and bestowing ere He commands and requires, it is profitable to hold the image of the man's evil in all its ugliness close up to his eyes; and so the bald facts are repeated next in the fewest, strongest words. Nor can the message close until a rigid law of retribution has been proclaimed, the slow operation of which will filter bitterness and shame through all his life.

"And David said unto Nathan, I have sinned against the Lord." Two words (in the Hebrew) make the transition from sullen misery to real though shaded peace. No lengthened outpouring, no accumulation of self-reproach; he is too deeply moved for many words, which he knows God does not need. More would have been less. All is contained in that one sob, in which the whole frostwork of these weary months breaks up and rolls away, swept before the strong flood. And as brief and simple as the confession, is the response, "And Nathan said unto David, The Lord also hath put away thy sin." How full and unconditional the blessing bestowed in these few words; how swift and sufficient the answer! So the long estrangement is ended. Thus simple and divine is the manner of pardon. In such short compass may the turning point of a life lie! But while confession and forgiveness heal the breach between God and David, pardon is not impunity, and the same sentence which bestows the remission of sin announces the exaction of a penalty. The judgments threatened a moment before—a moment so far removed now to David's consciousness that it would look as if an age had passed—are not withdrawn, and another is added, the death of Bathsheba's infant. God loves His servants too well to "suffer sin upon them," and the freest forgiveness and the happiest consciousness of it may consist with the loving infliction and the submissive bearing of pains, which are no longer the strokes of an avenging judge, but the chastisements of a gracious father.

The fifty-first psalm must, we think, be conceived of as following soon after Nathan's mission. There may be echoes of the prophet's stern question, "Wherefore hast thou despised the commandment of the Lord, to do evil in His sight?" and of the confession, "I have sinned against the Lord," in the words, "Against Thee, Thee only have I sinned, and done evil in Thy sight" (ver. 4), though perhaps the expressions are not so peculiar as to make the allusion certain. But, at all events, the penitence and prayers of the psalm can scarcely be supposed to have preceded the date of the historical narrative, which clearly implies that the rebuke of the seer was the first thing that broke up the dumb misery of unrepented sin.

Although the psalm is one long cry for pardon and restoration, one can discern an order and progress in its petitions—the order, not of an artificial reproduction of a past mood of mind, but the instinctive order in which the emotion of contrite desire will ever pour itself forth. In the psalm all begins, as all begins in fact, with the grounding of the cry for favor on "Thy loving-kindness," "the multitude of Thy tender mercies;" the one plea that avails with God, whose love is its own motive and its own measure, whose past acts are the standard for all His future, whose compassions, in their innumerable numbers, are more than the sum of our transgressions, though these be "more than the hairs of our head." Beginning with God's mercy, the penitent soul can learn to look next upon its own sin in all its aspects of evil. The depth and intensity of the psalmist's loathing of self is wonderfully expressed in his words for his crime. He speaks of his "transgressions" and of his "sin." Looked at in one way, he sees the separate acts of which he had been guilty—lust, fraud, treachery, murder: looked at in another, he sees them all knotted together, in one inextricable tangle of forked, hissing tongues, like the serpent locks that coil and twist round a Gorgon head. No sin dwells alone; the separate acts have a common root, and the whole is matted together like the green growth on a stagnant pond, so that, by whatever filament it is grasped, the whole mass is drawn towards you. And a profound insight into the essence and character of sin lies in the accumulated synonyms. It is "transgression," or, as the word might be rendered, "rebellion"—not the mere breach of an impersonal law, not merely an infraction of "the constitution of our nature"—but the rising of a subject will against its true king, disobedience to a person as well as contravention of a standard. It is "iniquity"—perversion or distortion—a word which expresses the same metaphor as is found in many languages, namely, crookedness as descriptive of deeds which depart from the perfect line of right. It is "sin," *i.e.*, "missing one's aim"; in which profound word is contained the truth that all sin is a blunder, shooting wide of the true goal, if regard be had to the end of our being, and not less wide if regard be had to our happiness. It ever misses the mark; the epitaph might be written over every sinner who seeks pleasure at the price of righteousness, "Thou fool."

Nor less pregnant with meaning is the psalmist's emphatic acknowledgment, "Against Thee, Thee only have I sinned." He is not content with looking upon his evil in itself, or in relation only to the people who had suffered by it; he thinks of it in relation to God. He had been guilty of crimes against Bathsheba and Uriah, and even the rough soldier whom he made his tool, as well as against his whole subjects; but, dark as these were, they assumed their true character only when they were discerned as done against God. "Sin," in its full sense, implies "God" as its correlative. We transgress against each other, but we sin against Him.

Nor does the psalmist stop here. He has acknowledged the tangled multiplicity and dreadful unity of his evil, he has seen its inmost character, he has learned to bring his deed into connection with God; what remains still to be confessed? He laments, and that not as extenuation (though it be explanation), but as aggravation, the sinful nature in which he had been born. The deeds had come from a source—a bitter fountain had welled out this blackness. He himself is evil, therefore he has done evil. The sin is his; he will not contest his full responsibility; and its foul characteristics declare the inward foulness from which it has flowed—and that foulness is himself. Does he therefore think that he is less to blame? By no means. His acknowledgment of an evil nature is the very deepest of his confessions, and leads not to a palliation of his guilt, but to a cry to Him who alone can heal the inward wound; and as He can purge away the transgressions, can likewise stanch their source, and give him to feel within "that he is healed from that plague."

The same intensity of feeling expressed by the use of so many words for sin is revealed also in the reiterated synonyms for pardon. The prayer comes from his lips over and over again, not because he thinks that he shall be heard for his much speaking, but because of the earnestness of his longing. Such repetitions are signs of the persistence of faith, while others, though they last like the prayers of Baal's priests, "from morning till the time of the evening sacrifice," indicate only the suppliant's doubt. David prays that his sins may be "blotted out," in which petition they are conceived as recorded against him in the archives of the heavens; that he may be "washed" from them, in which they are conceived as foul stains upon himself, needing for their removal hard rubbing and beating (for such is, according to some commentators, the force of the word); that he may be "cleansed"—the technical word for the priestly cleansing of the leper, and declaring him clear of the taint. He also, with similar recurrence to the Mosaic symbols, prays that he may be "purged with hyssop." There is a pathetic appropriateness in the petition, for not only lepers, but those who had become defiled by contact with a dead body, were thus purified; and on whom did the taint of corruption cleave as on the murderer of Uriah? The prayer, too, is even more remarkable in the original, which employs a verb formed from the word for "sin"; "and if in our language that were a word in use it might be translated, "Thou shalt un-sin me."

In the midst of these abased confessions and cries for pardon there comes with wonderful force and beauty the bold prayer for restoration to "joy and gladness"—an indication surely of more than ordinary confidence in the full mercy of God, which would efface all the consequences of his sin.

And following upon them are petitions for sanctifying, reiterated and many-sided, like those that have preceded. Three pairs of clauses contain these, in each of which the second member of the clause asks for the infusion into his spirit of some grace from God—that he may possess a "steadfast spirit," "Thy Holy Spirit," "a willing spirit." It is perhaps not an accident that the central petition of the three is the one which most clearly expresses the thought which all imply—that the human spirit can only be renewed and hallowed by the entrance into it of the Divine. We are not to commit the theological anachronism which has been applied with such evil effect to the whole Old Testament, and suppose that David meant by that central clause in his prayer for renewal all that we mean by it; but he meant, at least, that his spiritual nature could be made to love righteousness and hate iniquity by none other power than God's breathing on it. If we may venture to regard this as the heart of the series, the other two on either side of it may be conceived as its consequences. It will then be "a right spirit," or, as the word means, a steadfast spirit, strong to resist, not swept away by surges of passion, nor shaken by terrors of remorse, but calm, tenacious, and resolved, pressing on in the path of holiness, and immovable with the immobility of those who are rooted in God and goodness. It will be a free, or "a willing spirit," ready for all joyful service of thankfulness, and so penetrated with the love of his God that he will delight to do His will, and carry the law charactered in the spontaneous impulses of his renewed nature. Not without profound meaning does the psalmist seem to recur in his hour of penitence to the tragic fate of his predecessor in the monarchy, to whom, as to himself, had been given by the same anointing, the same gift of "the Spirit of God." Remembering how the holy chrism had faded from the raven locks of Saul long before his bloody head had been sent round Philistine cities to glut their revenge, and knowing that if God were "strict to mark iniquity," the gift which had been withdrawn from Saul would not be continued to himself, he prays, not as anointed monarch only, but as sinful man, "Take not Thy Holy Spirit from me." As before he had ventured to ask for the joy of forgiveness, so now he pleads once more for "the joy of Thy salvation," which comes from cleansing, from conscious fellowship—which he had so long and deeply felt, which for so many months had been hid from him by the mists of his own sin. The psalmist's natural buoyancy, the gladness which was an inseparable part of his religion, and had rung from his harp in many an hour of peril, the bold width of his desires, grounded on the clear breadth of his faith in God's perfect forgiveness, are all expressed in such a prayer from such lips at such a time, and may well be pondered and imitated by us.

The lowly prayer which we have been tracing rises ere its close to a vow of renewed praise. It is very beautiful to note how the poet nature, as well as the consciousness of a Divine function, unite in the resolve that crowns the psalm. To David no tribute that he could bring to God seemed so little unworthy—none to himself so joyous—as the music of his harp, and the melody of his songs; nor was any part of his kingly office so lofty in his estimation as his calling to proclaim in glowing words the name of the Lord, that men might learn to love. His earliest song in exile had closed with a like vow. It had been well fulfilled for many a year; but these last doleful months had silenced all his praise. Now, as hope begins to shine upon him once more, the frost which had stilled the stream of his devotion is melting, and as he remembers his glad songs of old, and this miserable dumbness, his final prayer is, "O Lord, open Thou my lips, and my mouth shall show forth Thy praise."

The same consciousness of sin, which we have found in a previous verse discerning the true significance of ceremonial purification, leads also to the recognition of the insufficiency of outward sacrifices—a thought which is not, as some modern critics would fain make it, the product of the latest age of Judaism, but appears occasionally through the whole of the history, and indicates not the date, but the spiritual elevation of its utterer. David sets it on the very summit of his psalm, to sparkle there like some stone of price. The rich jewel which he has brought up from the abyss of degradation is that truth which has shone out from its setting here over three millenniums: "The sacrifices of God are a broken spirit; a broken and contrite heart, O God, Thou wilt not despise."

The words which follow, containing a prayer for the building up of Zion, and a prediction of the continuous offering of sacrifice, present some difficulty. They do not necessarily presuppose that Jerusalem is in ruins; for "build Thou the walls" would be no less appropriate a petition if the fortifications were unfinished (as we know they were in David's time) than if they had been broken down. Nor do the words contradict the view of sacrifice just given, for the use of the symbol and the conviction of its insufficiency co-existed, in fact, in every devout life, and may well be expressed side by side. But the transition from so intensely personal emotions to intercession for Zion seems almost too sudden even for a nature as wide and warm as David's. If the closing verses are his, we may, indeed, see in them the king re-awaking to a sense of his responsibilities, which he had so long neglected, first, in the selfishness of his heart, and then in the morbid self-absorption of his remorse; and the lesson may be a precious one that the first thought of a pardoned man should be for others. But there is much to be said, on the other hand, in favor of the conjecture that these verses are a later addition, probably after the return from captivity, when the walls of Zion were in ruins, and the altar of the temple had been long cold. If so, then our psalm, as it came from David's full heart, would be all of a piece—one great gush of penitence and faith, beginning with, "Have mercy upon me, O God," ending with the assurance of acceptance, and so remaining for all ages the chart of the thorny and yet blessed path that leads "from death unto life." In that aspect, what it does not contain is as noteworthy as what it does. Not one word asks for exemption from such penalties of his great fall as can be inflicted by a loving Father on a soul that lives in His love. He cries for pardon, but he gives his back to the smiters whom God may please to send.

The other psalm of the penitent (32) has been already referred to in connection with the autobiographical materials which it contains. It is evidently of a later period than the fifty-first. There is no struggle in it; the prayer has been heard, and this is the beginning of the fulfilment of the vow to show forth God's praise. In the earlier he had said, "Then will I teach transgressors the way"; here he says, "I will instruct thee and teach thee in the way which though shalt go." There he began with the plaintive cry for mercy; here with a burst of praise celebrating the happiness of the pardoned penitent. There we heard the sobs of a man in the very agony of abasement; here we have the story of their blessed issue. There we had multiplied synonyms for sin, and for the forgiveness which was desired; here it is the many-sided preciousness of forgiveness possessed which runs over in various yet equivalent phrases. There the highest point to which he could climb was the assurance that a bruised heart was accepted, and the bones broken might still rejoice. Here the very first word is of blessedness, and the close summons the righteous to exuberant joy. The one is a psalm of wailing; the other, to use its own words, a "song of deliverance."

VICTORY IN FAILURE

What glad consciousness that he himself is the happy man whom he describes rings in the melodious variations of the one thought of forgiveness in the opening words! How gratefully he draws on the treasures of that recent experience, while he sets forth as being the "taking away" of sin, as if it were the removal of a solid something, or the lifting of a burden off his back; and as the "covering" of sin, as if it were the wrapping of its ugliness in thick folds that hide it for ever even from the all-seeing Eye; and as the "non-reckoning" of sin, as if it were the discharge of a debt! What vivid memory of past misery in the awful portrait of his impenitent self, already referred to—on which the mind dwells in silence, while the musical accompaniment (as directed by the "selah") touches some plaintive minor or grating discord! How noble and eloquent the brief words (echo of the historical narrative) that tell the full and swift forgiveness that followed simple confession—and how effectively the music again comes in, prolonging the thought and rejoicing in the pardon! How sure he is that his experience is of priceless value to the world for all time, when he sees in his absolution of motive that will draw all the godly nearer to their Helper in heaven! How full his heart is of praise, that he cannot but go back again to his own story, and rejoice in God his hiding-place—whose past wondrous love assures him that in the future songs of deliverance will ring him round, and all his path be encompassed with music of praise.

So ends the more personal part of the psalm. A more didactic portion follows, the generalization of that. Possibly the voice which now speaks is a higher than David's. "I will instruct thee and teach thee in the way which thou shalt go. I will guide thee with mine eyes," scarcely sounds like words meant to be understood as spoken by him. They are the promise from heaven of a gentle teaching to the pardoned man, which will instruct by no severity, but by patient schooling; which will direct by no harsh authority, but by that loving glance that is enough for those who love, and is all too subtle and delicate to be perceived by any other. Such gracious direction is not for the psalmist alone, but it needs a spirit in harmony with God to understand it. For others there can be nothing higher than mere force, the discipline of sorrow, the bridle in the hard mouth, the whip for the stiff back. The choice for all men is through penitence and forgiveness to rise to the true position of men, capable of receiving and obeying a spiritual guidance, which appeals to the heart, and gently subdues the will, or by stubborn impenitence to fall to the level of brutes, that can only be held in by a halter and driven by a lash. And because this is the alternative, therefore "Many sorrows shall be to the wicked; but he that trusteth in the Lord, mercy shall compass him about."

And then the psalm ends with a great cry of gladness, three times reiterated, like the voice of a herald on some festal day of a nation: "Rejoice in Jehovah! and leap for joy, O righteous! and gladly shout, all ye upright in heart!"

Such is the end of the sobs of the penitent.

VICTORY OVER DARKNESS

Arise, shine, for thy light is come, and the glory of the Lord has risen upon thee.

(ISA. 60:1)

THE PERSONATION OF ISRAEL as a woman runs through the second half of Isaiah's prophecy. We see her thrown on the earth a mourning mother, a shackled captive. We hear her summoned once and again to awake, to arise, to shake herself from the dust, to loose the bands of her neck. These summonses are prophecies of the impending Messianic deliverances,

The same circle of truths, in a somewhat different aspect, is presented in the verses before us. The prophet sees the earth wrapped in a funeral pall of darkness and a beam of more than natural light falling on one prostrate form; the old story is repeated, Zion sits in the light while Egypt cowers in gloom. The light which shines upon her is the glory of the Lord, the ancient brightness that dwelt between the cherubim within the veil in the secret place of the most High, and is now come out into the open world to envelop the desolate captive. Thus touched by the light she becomes light, and in her turn is bidden to shine. There is a very remarkable correspondence reiterated in my text between the illuminating God and the illuminated Zion. The word for shine is connected with the word for light and might fairly be rendered "lighten" or "be light." Twice the phrase "the light" is employed; once to mean the light which is thine because it shines on thee; once to mean the light which is thine because it shines from thee. The other word, three times repeated, for *rising*, is the technical word which expresses the sunrise, and it is applied both to the flashing glory that falls upon Zion, and to the light that gleams from her. Touched by the sun she becomes a sun, and blazes in her heaven in a splendor that draws men's hearts.

Beneath the poetry of my text there lie very definite conceptions of a very solemn and grave character, and these conceptions are the foundation of the ringing summons that follows and which reposes upon a double basis—viz. *"for* thy light is come," and *"for* darkness covers the earth." There is a double element in the representation. We have a darkened earth and a sunlit and sun-like church, and unless we hold these two convictions—both of them—in firm grasp, and that not merely as convictions that influence our understanding, but as ever present forces acting on our emotions, our consciences, our wills, we shall not do the work God has set us to do in the world. I need not dwell long on the former of these, or speak of that funeral pall that wraps the whole earth. Only remember it is no darkness that came from His hand who forms the light and creates darkness, but is like the smoke that lies over Sheffield—the work of many an earth born fire, whose half consumed foulness hides the sun from us. It we take the sulphurous and smoky pall that wraps the earth and analyze its contents, they are these: the darkness of ignorance, the darkness of sorrow, the darkness of sin. Of ignorance, for over all the wide regions that lie beneath that covering spread over all nations, is there any certitude about God, about man, about morals, about responsibilities, about eternity? Peradventures, guesses, dreams, precious fragments of truth, twisted into the worst of lights, noble aspirations side by side with jestural representations. These are the things on which our brethren repose or try to repose. We do not forget that light which lighteneth every man that cometh into the world. We do not forget,

Victory over Darkness

of course, that everywhere there are feelings after Him, and everywhere there are gleams and glimpses of a vanishing light, else life were impossible; but, oh, dear brethren, let us not forget that the people sit in darkness of ignorance which is the saddest darkness that can afflict men.

And it is a darkness of sorrow, for all the ills that flesh is heir to press unalleviated and unsustained by any known helper in the heavens upon millions of our fellows. They stand, as the great German poet describes himself as standing, in one of the most pathetic of his lyrics, before the marble image of the fair goddess with beauty on her face and beauty raying from her limbs, but she has no arms. So tears fall undried. The light-hearted savage is a fiction. What a heavy gloom lies upon the past and the present which darkens into an impenetrable fog, which wraps and hides the future.

And the darkness is a darkness of sin as well as of sorrow and of ignorance. On that point I need not dwell. We all believe that all have sinned and come short of the glory of God, and we all believe that idolatry, as we see it, and as it is wrought out, is an ally of impurity and of sin. The process is this; men make gods in their own image, and the gods make devils of the men. "They that make them are like unto them, so is every one that trusteth in them." We need no other principle than that to account for the degradation of heathenism and for the obscenities and foul transgression within the very courts of the temple.

Now, let me urge you in one sentence to be on your guard against present day tendencies which weaken the force of this solemn, tragical conviction about the realities of heathendom. The new science of comparative religion has done much for us. I am not saying one word against

VICTORY IN FAILURE

this pursuit, or the conclusions which are drawn from it. But I want you to remember that the underlying truths buried beneath the system that any men hold as their religion are one thing, and the practical working of the system as we see it in daily life is altogether another. The actual character of heathenism is not to be learned from the sacred books of all nations and the precious gleams of wisdom and feelings after the Divine which we recognise in man. As a simple matter of fact all over the world the religion of heathen nations is a mass of obscenity, intertwined so closely with nobler thoughts that the two seem to be inseparable. Unalleviated sorrows, bestial foulnesses, a gross ignorance covering all the most important realities for men—these are the facts with which we have to grapple. Do not let us forget them.

And on the other side, remember the contrasted picture here of the sunlit and sunny church. The incarnation of Jesus Christ is the fulfillment of my text. We behold His glory, the glory as of the only begotten of the Father, full of grace and truth. If you and I are Christians, we are bound to believe in Him as the exclusive source of certainty. We hear from Him no Peradventure, but His word is "Verily, verily, I say unto thee," and on that we rest all our knowledge of God, of duty, of man, and of the future. Instead of fears, doubts, perhapses, we have a living Christ and His rock Word. And in Him is all joy and in Him is the cleansing from all sin. And this three-fold radiance, into which the one pure light may be analyzed, falls upon us. It falls all over the world as well; but they into whose hearts it has come, they whose faces are turned to it, they receive it in a sense which the unreceptive and unresponsive darkness of the world does not. The light shineth in the darkness, and the darkness will have none of it, and so it is darkness yet. The light shineth upon us, and if by His mercy we have opened our hearts to it, then, according to the profound teaching of this context, we are not only a sun-lighted, but a sunlike Church, and to us the commandment comes, "Arise, shine, for thy light is come, and has turned thy poor darkness into a sun too."

If we have the light we shall be light. That is but putting in a picturesque form the very central truth of Christianity. The last word of the Gospel is transformation. We become like Him if we live near to Him, and the end for which the Master became like unto us in His incarnation and passion, was that we might become like to Him by the reception of His very own life unto our souls. Light makes many a surface on which it falls flash, but it is the rays which are not absorbed that are reflected in the optics of earth, but in this loftier region the deviation is not superficial but inward, and it is the light which is swallowed up within us that then comes forth from us. Christ will dwell in our hearts, and we shall be like some poor little diamond-shaped bit of glass in a cottage window which, when the sun smites it, is visible over miles of the plain. And if that sun falls upon us, its image will be mirrored in our hearts, and flashing in our lives. The clouds that lie over the sunset, though in themselves they be but poor, gray and moist vapor, when smitten by its beneficent radiance become not unworthy ministers and attendants upon its glory. So, my brethren, it may be with us, for Christ comes to be our light. Because He is in us and with us, we are changed into His likeness, and the names that are most appropriate to Him He shares with us. Is He the "Son"? We are sons. Is He "the Light of the word"? His own lips tell us: "Ye are the light of the world." Is He the Christ? The Psalm says: "Touch not my Christs, and do

VICTORY IN FAILURE

My prophets no harm." Critics have quarrelled over these last chapters of the Book of Isaiah, as to who the servant of the Lord is; whether it is the personal or collective Israel, whether it is Christ or His Church. Let us take the lesson that He and we are so united, that His offices, all but the one office that made the union possible, wherein He was sacrificed on the cross for us all—belong by derivation to His servants, and that He, the Sun of Righteousness, moves in the heavens circled by many another sun. So, dear friends, these two convictions of these two facts, the dark earth, the sunlit, sun-like church, lie at the basis of all our missionary work. If once we begin to doubt about them, if once we begin to think that men have got a good deal of light already, and can do very well without much more, or, if we at all are hesitant about our possession of the light, and the certitudes and the joys that are in it, then goodbye to your missionary zeal. We shall soon begin to ask the question, To what purpose is this waste? though the lips that first asked it, by-the-bye, did not much recommend it, and shall consider that money and resources and precious lives are too precious to be thrown away thus. But if we rightly appreciate the force of these twin principles, then we shall be ready to listen to the ringing summons.

We have here in the second place based upon these two facts the summons to the church: "Shine, for thy light is come." If we have light, we are light. If we are light we shall shine; but the shining is not altogether spontaneous and effortless. Stars do not need to be bidden to shine nor candles either; but we need the exhortation because there are many things that thwart the brilliance and the clearance of our minds. The light is light which radiated; the only effect light has is to shine, and the silent wings witness of a Christian transformed into the likeness of Jesus Christ is, perhaps, the best contribution that any of us can make to the spread of His kingdom. It is with us as it is with the great lights in the heavens. There is no speech nor language; their voice is not heard, yet their line has gone through all the earth, and their words to the end of the world. So we may quietly ray out the light in us and witness the transforming power of our Master by the transparent purity of our lives. But then the command suggests likewise effort, and the effort may be in the direction of the specific vocal proclamation of His name. I take both these methods of fulfilling the command into my view, in the further remarks that I make, and I put that which I have to say upon this into three sentences: If we are light, we shall be able to shine; if we are light, we are bound to shine; if we are light, we shall want to shine. We shall be able to shine. Any man can manifest what he is unless he is a coward. Any man can talk about the things that are interesting to him if only they are interesting to him. Any man that has Jesus Christ can say so; and perhaps the utterance of the simple personal conviction is the best method of proclaiming His name. All other things are surplusage. They are good when they come, they may be done without. Learning eloquence, and the like of these are the adornments of the lamp, but it does not matter whether the lamp be a gorgeous affair of gilt and richness, or whether it be a poor piece of block tin; the main question is: are there wick and oil in it? The pitcher may be gold and silver, or costly crystal marble, or it may be a poor potsherd. Never mind. If there is water in it, it will be precious to a thirsty lip. And so, dear brethren, though it has not directly to do with foreign missions, my purpose this morning is far more to rouse each of us to a consciousness of our personal responsibility wherever those influences extend, and I press this upon you— every Christain man has the power, if he be a Christian, to proclaim his Master, and if he has the Light will be able to show it. I pause for a moment to say that this suggests for us the condition of all faithful and effectual witnesses for Jesus Christ. Cultivate understanding and all other faculties as much as you like; but, oh! you Christian ministers, as well as others in less official and public positions, remember this, the fitness to impart is to possess, and that being taken for granted the main thing is secured. As long as the electric light is in contact with the battery so long does it burn. Electricians have been trying during the past few years to make accumulators, things in which they can store the influence and put it away in a corner and use it so that the light need not be in connection with the battery; and they have not succeeded; at least, it is only a very partial success. You and I cannot start accumulators. Let us remember personal contact is power and only the personal contact. Arise, shine, but oh! if thou hast gone out of the light, thou wilt shine no more.

Well then, again, if we are light we are bound to shine. That is an obvious principle. The capacity to shine is the obligation to shine, for we are all knit together by such mystical cords in this strange brotherhood of humanity that every one of us holds his position as trust property for the use and behoof of others, and in the present case that which we have received and the price at which we have received it gives an edge to the keenness of the obligation, and adds a new band to the stringency of the command. It is because Christ has given Himself thus to us that the possession of Him binds us to the imitation of His example, and the impartation of Him to all our brethren. The obligation lies at our doors and cannot be delegated or devolved.

If we have light we shall wish to shine. What shall we say about the Christian people that never really had such a wish? God forbid that I should say they have no light; but this I will say, it burns very dimly. Dear brethren, there is no better test of the depth and the purity of our personal attachment to, and possession of our master than the impulse that will spring from them to communicate them to others. "Necessity is laid upon me, yea, woe is me if I preach not." That should be the word of every one of us, and it will be in the measure in which we ourselves get thoroughly hold of Jesus Christ. "This is a day of good tidings. We cannot hold our peace," said the handful of lepers in the camp, "if we are silent some mischief will come to us." "Thy word when I shut it up in my bones and said I will speak no more in Thy name, was like a fire, and I was weary of forebearing and I could not stay." Do you know anything of the Divine necessity to share your blessing with the men around you? Did you ever feel what it was to carry a burden of the Lord that drove you to speech, and left you no rest until you had done what it has impelled you to do? If not, I beseech you ask yourselves whether you cannot get nearer to the sun than away out yonder on the very edge of its system, receiving so few of its beams, and these so impotent that they can scarcely do more than melt the surface of the thick ribbed ice that wraps your spirit. If we are light we shall be enabled, we shall be bound, we shall wish to shine. Christian men and women, is this true of you?

Lastly, notice here the confident promise, "The Gentiles shall come to Thy light, and kings to the brightness of Thy rising." If we have the light we shall be light; if we are light we shall shine, and if we shine we shall attract. Certainly men and women with the light of Christ in them will draw men to them just as many an eye that cannot look undazzled upon the sun, can look upon it mirrored upon some polished surface. A painter will fling upon his canvas a scene that you and I, with our purblind eyes, have looked at hundreds of times and seen no beauty in it, but when we gaze on the picture then we see how fair it is. There is an attractive power in the light of Christ shining from the face of a man. Of course, we have to moderate our expectations. We have to remember that whilst it is true that men will come to the light, it is also true that men love the darkness, and will not come to the light because their deeds are evil; and we have to remember that we have no right to anticipate rapid results. "An inheritance may be begotten hastily at the beginning, but the latter end thereof shall not be blessed," said the wise man, and the history of the Christian Church in many of its missionary operations is a sad commentary upon the saying. We must remember that we cannot estimate how long the preparation for a change which will be developed swiftly, may be. The sun on these autumn mornings shines upon the fog, and the people below, because there is a fog, do not know that it is shining, but it is doing its work on the upper layer all the while, and at length eats its way through the fleecy obstruction, which then swiftly disappears. That must be a very, very long day of which the morning twilight has been eighteen hundred years. Therefore although the vision tarries, we may fall back with unswerving confidence on these words of my text—"The Gentiles shall come to the brightness of Thy rising."

But after all this has been said, are you satisfied with the rate of progress? Are you satisfied with the swiftness of the fulfilment of such hopes? Whose fault is it that the rate of progress is what it is? Yours and mine and our predecessors. There is such a thing as hasting the day of the Lord, and there is such a thing as protracting the time of waiting. Dear brethren, the secret of our slow growth at home and abroad lies in my text. Fulfill the conditions and you will get the result; but if you are not shining by a light which is Christ's light, who promised that *it* would have attraction or draw men to it? A great deal of the work of the Christian Church—but do not let us hide ourselves in the generality of that word—a great deal of *our* work is artificial light, brewed out of retorts, and smelling sulphurous; and a great deal more of it is the phosphoresence that glimmers above decay. If the Christian Church has ceased in any measure, or any of its members,. to be able to attract by the exhibition of its right light which the Christian Church set down, perhaps it will find a reason for its failure. It is Christ, the holy Christ, the loving Christ, the Christ in us making us wise and gentle, it is the Christ manifested by word and by work, that will draw the nations to Him. So, men and brethren, do you keep near your Master and live close by His side till you are drenched and saturated with His glory, and all your poor cold vapors turned into visible divinity and manifested Jesus. Keep near to Him. As long as a bit of scrap iron touches a magnet, it *is* a magnet. As soon as the contact is broken it ceases to attract. If you live in the full sunshine of Christ and have Him not merely playing upon the surface of your mind, but sinking deep down into it and transforming your whole being, then some men will, as they look at you, be filled with strange longings, and will say: "Come, let us walk in the light of the Lord." So may you and I live, like the morning star, which, from its serene altitudes, touched into radiance by the sun unseen from the darkened plains, prophecies its rising to a sleeping world, and is content to be lost in the luster of that unsetting Light!

FAITH IS THE VICTORY

Like precious faith with us.
(II PETER 1:1)

CERTAIN CHARACTERISTIC PHRASES appear in both the Epistles written by the Apostle Peter.

This word "precious" is one of these. We read in the first Epistle of "the trial of your faith being much more precious than of gold that perisheth, though it be tried with fire." And a few verses further on, we read, of "the precious blood of Christ." In the next chapter we have a quotation from Isaiah interpreted of Christ—"A chief corner-stone, elect, precious," which "preciousness," according to the more accurate rendering of the Revised Version, is in the next verse said to belong to believers. In the second Epistle we find the phrase "like precious faith," and in an immediately following verse we read of "exceeding great and precious promises."

Thus there runs through both letters the use of the same characteristics and somewhat indefinite epithet, which expresses only the Apostle's lofty idea of the value of the themes with which he is dealing. The old man getting near the end of his life had come to think that the really valuable things were not the things which can be handled, counted and weighed; that the truly precious things were these—Christ, His blood, God's promises, and the faith which grasps these three. These are worth all the rest; and as for the rest—well, if you have them you are not much the better, and if you have not them you are very little the worse.

But my text not only speaks of "*precious* faith," but of "*like precious* faith with us." And the question is, who are the two classes whose faith is here declared to be of equal worth? One answer may be that the "us" means Peter and his brother Apostles, and if so, then we have here a declaration of the substantial identity and equal value of the faith of all Christian people, whether they hold the highest office or fill the most undistinguished place in the Church.

But more probably the two classes referred to here are the Gentile Christians to whom the letter was addressed, and the Jewish Christians, with whom Peter classes himself. In the name of all the latter he welcomes the "uncircumcision" into the unity of the Church, and recognises them as possessors of the same faith, and, therefore, enriched with the same salvation. He proclaims that the wall of partition is broken down, and stretches his hand across its ruins to grasp his brethren's hands. He is back again to the old lesson which he learned on the house-top at Joppa and in the dwelling of Cornelius. It is the reiteration of his own argument with which he had quieted the suspicions of the Church at Jerusalem when they heard of his baptism of Cornelius. "Forasmuch then as God gave them the like gift as He did unto us, who believed in the Lord Jesus Christ, what was I, that I could withstand God?" Although the old national bigotry had conquered him for awhile, and he had been unfaithful to his earlier convictions, he has returned to them, and is side by side with "his beloved brother Paul" in the assertion of the abolition of all national prerogative, and the inclusion on equal terms within the Church of all men, be they of what race they may, if only they possess faith in Jesus Christ.

Such being the force and bearing of these words, we may use them as suggesting some not unimportant points, which throw light upon that much spoken about, but often dimly understood, subject of Faith, especially in regard of its object, its value, and its substantial identity under the most different forms.

Consider then, first, the object of faith, as here defined.

The Authorized Version reads, "To them that have obtained like precious faith with us *through* the righteousness of God and of our Saviour Jesus Christ." But the Revised Version reads more accurately, "faith. . . . *in* the righteousness." The former rendering is admissible, and would give the meaning that God's righteousness revealed in Jesus Christ gave occasion for our faith, which would be quite true, inasmuch as if there had been no righteousness revealed, there could have been no faith. But that meaning is less satisfactory than the other, which regards the righteousness as being the object of our faith. As Paul says, "The righteousness of God from faith is revealed unto faith."

Now the object of faith is much more frequently said in the New Testament to be Jesus Christ, and it is all-important to keep clearly in view that He, the personal Christ, is the true and proper object of our faith. Faith is trust, and the object of trust must be a person. We may say that we trust a promise, but that really means that we trust him who has made it. We may believe a creed, but for trust we must have a living God of Whom the creed speaks. It is Christ Himself, then, in the sweetness and graciousness of His character, in the sacrifice of His death, and in the glory of His risen life, Whom we trust in, and by trusting in Whom we live.

That principle is important as bringing clearly into view how faith in Christ is strictly parallel with our trust in one another. It is the very same act which knits

VICTORY IN FAILURE

us to Christ, and to God in Christ, and which knits us to one another. It is faith which makes it possible that the world should go on at all. The same confidence with which men of business rely upon each other in their transactions, the same confidence with which we in our families safely trust in the love and truth of wife or husband, friend or child, when directed to Jesus Christ becomes the spring and the heart of all religion.

What tragic folly and waste it is that we should squander the treasure of our trust on such unworthy objects, when we might safely lodge it in the safe keeping of His Almighty hands! The vine which trails along the ground and twines its tendrils round any rubbish which it may come upon, is sure to be trodden under foot. If it lift itself from the earth and fling its clasping rings round the shaft of the Cross, its stem will not be bruised, and its clusters will be heavier and sweeter. The tendrils which anchor it to the rubbish heap are the same as those which clasp it to the Cross. The trust with which we lean upon the bruised reeds of human help is the same as that with which we lean upon the iron pillar of a Saviour's aid. Faith is trust, and its object is not a creed, but a person, whom it is the work of all creeds to make known.

That being understood, then comes the importance of the words of my text. A man may say: "Oh! I trust in Christ, I am a Christian"; but the whole question is: What Christ is it that you are trusting in, and what is it that you are trusting to Him for? So, in order to make definite the vagueness which may attach to the thought of faith in a person, unless we declare what the person is, we have to keep in view such sayings as this of my text. The Apostle Paul, for example, speaks in one

Faith Is the Victory

place of "faith in His blood," and his brother Peter here speaks of "faith in the righteousness of God and Christ." If we take these two definitions of the object of faith, they explain what true faith in Christ has to lay hold of. If you are truly trusting in Christ you are trusting in His blood; if you are truly trusting in Christ you are trusting in His righteousness. If your faith, so-called, lays hold on a Christ Whose blood is nothing to you, Whose righteousness is to you only example and stimulus, and no more, my brother! you have not got the "like precious faith" with those of whom the Apostle is the representative. The Christ Whom we must trust is the Christ Whose blood cleanses from all sin, Whose righteousness makes us righteous. And the great truths that He, by His perfect obedience, has fulfilled the law, that by His death we are justified, and that by His indwelling in us we are sanctified, are all summed up in this word of my text, which declares the object of faith to be the righteousness of God and our Saviour Jesus Christ.

There is much need, I think, in these days, when so much foolish impatience of doctrine has crept into the professing Church, and when some men are so afraid of anything that savours of that great truth of a dying Christ Whose blood is our righteousness, to say plainly that not only must our faith grasp Jesus, but that our faith must grasp this Jesus,—the Jesus that died for our sins and was raised again for our justification—if we are ever to be "found in Him, not having our own righteousness, which is of the law, but that which is through the faith of Christ."

Now, still further consider the worth of this faith.

What is the value of faith? Why is it so precious? I have already pointed out that in both these letters certain things are declared to be precious, and I enumerated them as being Christ Himself, Christ's blood, and God's great promises. These are precious in one way by virtue of their own inherent value. But faith is only precious because of that which it lays hold of.

So that is the first item in the preciousness of faith—its worth as a *channel*. You remember that in one place we read about "the door of faith." What is the worth of a door? It is only a hole in a wall. The value of the door is in that which it admits or in that which it is the means of our entering into. So faith is precious, not because of anything in itself, for it is nothing in itself, but because of what it grips and grasps, and of what it admits into our hearts.

Just as the hand of a dyer that has been working with crimson will be crimson; just as the hand that has been holding fragrant perfumes will be perfumed; so my faith, which is only the hand by which I lay hold upon precious things, will take the tincture and the fragrance of what it grasps. A bit of earthenware piping may be worth a few pence in intrinsic value, but if it is the means by which water is brought into a besieged city which else would perish with thirst, who will estimate its worth? In like manner, faith is precious because it brings God in Christ, and the blood of Christ and the promises of Christ, all flooding into my soul to fill it with life, and fruitfulness, and refreshing. It is the hand which lays hold on the hand of God that He may hold me up. It is the taking down of the shutters that the sunshine may come in. Which lights the room, the removal of the shutters or the sunshine? Which is the precious thing, the faith or the Christ that rises on the faithful soul with "healing in His beams"? It is the grasping of the poles of the electric battery, powerful only as bringing me into contact with the quick and quickening impulse. Faith brings all riches to me, and therefore is itself gilded with some reflection of their luster, and partakes of their preciousness.

Then again we may consider the worth of faith as a *defense*. We read of the "shield of faith." How is faith valuable as a shield? Has it any power of protection in itself? Am I any the safer merely because I am confident that I am? A man may have an obstinate confidence which is misplaced and may lull him into a fatal security. I do not become safe by believing myself to be so, however strong may be the imagination or the fancy. All depends upon what it is that I am relying on. So, then, faith is no shield in itself; it has no power to protect you from anything, either from dangers without or dangers within. "The Lord God is a Sun and Shield. O Lord of Hosts, Blessed is the man that trusteth in Thee." Thrust your arm, howsoever feeble it may be, through the handles of that great Buckler, and hide yourself behind Him, and "He will cover your head in the day of battle."

Loose things on the deck of a ship will be blown overboard when the storm comes. There is only one way to keep them firm, and that is to lash them to something that is fixed. It is not the bit of rope that gives them security, but it is the stable thing to which they are lashed. Lash yourselves to Christ by faith, and whatever storm or tempest comes, you will be safe, and stand firm and immovable. Your faith is precious because it knits you to His immortal stability.

And in like manner we may consider the worth of faith as a *purifier*. When Peter had to defend himself before the Church in Jerusalem for his action in regard to

Cornelius, his one plea was, "God . . . put no difference between us and them, purifying their hearts by faith." But how does faith purify? Is there anything in my confidence which will make me pure? No! There is no moral efficacy in the mere act of trust. All depends upon what it is that you are trusting to. You will get like the object of your confidence. If you are trusting to money you will get jaundiced with it. If you are trusting to creatures, the great law will come true about you which has determined the degradation of all idolatrous nations: "they that make them are like unto them, so is every one that trusteth in them." As the man's trust, so will the man one day become. The only faith that purifies is faith in Him Who is pure. My faith makes me clean only in the measure in which, and because, it joins me to the Christ Who Himself is righteous, and gives me possession of all the motives to purity which love to Him can set in action, and of all the power for purifying which the gift of His Spirit can bring. Faith is the believing contemplation of Christ in His beauty and graciousness, and every man that hath this confidence in Him does purify himself, because He is pure. Faith is the believing appropriation of that Divine Spirit by Whose mighty operation alone we can become holy and good. And so, brethren, all the value of faith comes from the intrinsic and unspeakable preciousness of these things with which it is conversant.

And now, lastly, my text suggests to us the substantial identity and equal preciousness of faith in all varieties of form and degree.

If we adopt the view that the Apostle is here declaring, that the faith of the Gentile Christian is equally precious with that of the Jew, the door is opened for the recognition of the oneness of faith under the extremest differences of form.

Faith Is the Victory

There is no such gulf between any two sects of Christians who have faith in the blood and righteousness of Christ, as there was between the Gentile and the Jewish sections of the primitive Church at the time when this Epistle was written. And yet, says Peter, here is a bridge that can be thrown across that deep gulf, for on both sides of it faith may be identical. Let us learn that two men who both alike are trusting to Jesus Christ as their Saviour, and who are most unlike each other in all other respects, in creed, in culture, in general outlook on the world, in disposition and character, are liker each other than a Christian man and a non-Christian, who in all particulars except faith are as like as twins. The deepest thing in every man that has it is his faith in Jesus Christ, and likeness in that brings him near all others who have it, however unlike on the surface their characteristics may be.

But now do not let us run away with the lazy charity, so called, which is often mere poisonous indifference to truth. I will go as far as any man in recognising the substantial identity, under the most different forms of manifestation, of faith in Jesus Christ. The Quaker on that hand, who will have no ritual or ceremony at all, and the Roman Catholic priest on the other, on the steps of the altar, with the incense-smoke curling about him as he sings Mass, may be brothers. And all manner of differences in opinion, in politics, in culture, in race which may separate men from men, are like the cracks upon the surface of a bit of rock, which are an inch deep, while the solid mass goes down a thousand feet. But I am not going to pretend that the man whose Christ did not die for him, and whose Christ gives him no righteousness in which he can stand before God, possesses "like precious faith unto us." To say that he does is to worship charity at the expense of truth, and to be a traitor to the Master for the sake of seeming to be friendly with those who are not His subjects. The widest charity has no vagueness; all that love the Lord Jesus Christ in sincerity are one, but it must be the *Lord* Jesus Christ that they love.

And then in like manner, if my text have the other application to which I have adverted, that of the identity in faith between the Apostles and the humblest believers, that application teaches us the other lesson of the substantial identity of faith under all degrees of attainment. The poor man's half-sovereign, which stands between him and want—his "one ewe lamb," is made of the same gold as Rothschild's millions. Each tiny particle of a magnet, if it be smitten off the whole mass, is magnetic, and sends out influence from its two little poles. And so the smallest and the feeblest faith is one in character, and one in intrinsic value with the loftiest and superbest. Only, as is the measure of the man's faith, so will be the measure of his possession of the precious things.

Therefore, seeing that we may all have that faith which, whether it be as a grain of mustard-seed or whether it be grown to be greater than all herbs, is yet one in its mysterious life; seeing that we may all possess it, and that there are infinitely various degrees in which we may possess it, and consequently infinite increase possible in the good things it brings to us, let us all take that old prayer, and with it the always appropriate confession, "Lord! I believe, help Thou my unbelief." And then, like this very Apostle, if, standing upon the stormy billows, when our hearts are ready to fail us, we "stretch lame hands of faith," and grasp the strong Hand which will be stretched out to us, we shall be held up.

"Lord, help thou mine unbelief"

Faith Is the Victory

His strong hand, not my weakness; His grasp, not mine; Christ, not my faith in Christ, will keep me from falling and present me faultless before the presence of His glory.

THE GOOD NEWS OF GLORY

The glorious gospel of the blessed God
(I TIM. 1:11)

THE PROPER RENDERING is given in the Revised Version,—"the gospel of the glory," not the "glorious gospel." The Apostle is not telling us what kind of thing the Gospel is, but what it is about. He is dealing not with its quality but with its contents. It is a Gospel which reveals, has to do with, is the manifestation of, the glory of God.

The word "blessed," which is used here, and is only applied to God once more in Scripture, has no reference to the human attribution of blessing and praise to Him, but describes Him altogether apart from what men say of him, as what He is in Himself, the "blessed," or, as we might almost say, the "happy" God. If the word happy seems too trivial, suggesting ideas of levity, of turbulence, of possible change, then I do not know that we can find any better word than that which is already employed in my text, if only we remember that it means the solemn, calm, restful, perpetual gladness that fills the heart of God.

Take, first, that striking thought that the revelation of God in Jesus Christ is the glory of God.

The theme, or contents, or the purpose of the whole Gospel, is to set forth and make manifest to men the Glory of God.

Now what do we mean by "the glory"? I think, perhaps, that question may be most simply answered by remembering the definite meaning of the word in the Old Testament. There it designates, usually, that supernatural and lustrous light which dwelt between the cherubim, the symbol of the presence and of the self-manifestation of God. So that we may say, in brief, that the glory of God is the sum-total of the light that streams from His self-revelation, considered as being the object of adoration and praise by a world that gazes upon Him.

And if this be the notion of the glory of God, is it not a startling contrast which is suggested between the apparent contents and the real substance of that Gospel? Suppose a man, for instance, who had no previous knowledge of Christianity, being told that in it he would find the highest revelation of the glory of God. He comes to the Book, and finds that the very heart of it is not about God, but about a man; that this revelation of the glory of God is the biography of a man; and more than that, that the larger portion of that biography is the story of the humiliations, and the sufferings, and the death of the man. Would it not strike him as a strange paradox that the history of a *man's* life was the shining apex of all revelations of the glory of *God?* And yet so it is, and the Apostle, just because to him the Gospel was the story of the Christ Who lived and died, declares that in this story of a human life, patient, meek, limited, despised, rejected, and at last crucified, lies, brighter than all other flashings of the Divine light, the very heart of the luster and palpitating center and fontal source of all the radiance with which God has flooded the world. The history of Jesus Christ is the glory of God. And that involves two or three considerations on which I dwell briefly.

One of them is this: Christ, then, is the self-revelation of God. If, when we deal with the story of His life and death, we are dealing simply with the biography of a man, however pure, lofty, inspired he may be, then I ask what sort of connection there is between that biography which the four Gospels gives us, and what my text says is the substance of the Gospel? What force of logic is there in the Apostle's words: "God commendeth *His* love toward us in that whilst we were yet sinners *Christ* died for us," unless there is some altogether different connection between the God Who commends His love and the Christ who dies to commend it, than exists between a mere man and God? To deliver my text and a hundred other passages of Scripture from the charge of being extravagant nonsense and clear, illogical *non sequiturs*, you must believe that in that Man Christ Jesus "we behold His glory—the glory of the only begotten of the Father"; and that when we look—haply not without some touch of tenderness and awed admiration in our hearts—upon His gentleness we have to say, "the patient God"; when we look upon His tears we have to say, "the pitying God"; when we look upon His cross we have to say, "the redeeming God"; and gazing upon the Man, see in Him the manifest Divinity. Oh! Listen to that voice, "He that hath seen Me hath seen the Father," and bow before the story of the human life as being the revelation of the indwelling God.

And then, still further, my text suggests that this self-revelation of God in Jesus Christ is the very climax and highest point of all God's revelations to men. I believe that the loftiest exhibition and conception of the Divine character which is possible to us must be made to us in the form of a man. I believe that the law of humanity, for ever, in Heaven as on earth, is this, that the Son is the Revealer of God; and that no loftier—yea, at bottom, no other—communication of the Divine nature can be made to man than is made in Jesus Christ.

But be that as it may, let me urge upon you this thought, that in that wondrous story of the life and death of our Lord Jesus Christ the very high-water mark of Divine self-communication has been touched and reached. All the energies of the Divine nature are embodied there. The "riches, both of the *wisdom* and of the *knowledge* of God," are in the Cross and Passion of our Saviour. "To declare at this time his *righteousness*" Jesus Christ came to die. The Cross is "the *power* of God unto salvation." Or, to put it into other words, and avail oneself of an illustration, we know the old story of the queen who, for the love of an unworthy human heart, dissolved pearls in the cup and gave them to him to drink. We may say that God comes to us, and for the love of us, reprobate and unworthy, has melted all the jewels of His nature into that cup of blessing which He offers to us, saying: "Drink ye all of it." The whole God-head, so to speak, is smelted down to make that rushing river of molten love which flows from the Cross of Christ into the hearts of men. Here is the highest point of God's revelation of Himself.

And my text implies, still further, that the true living, flashing center of the glory of God is the love of God. Christendom is more than half heathen yet, and it betrays its heathenism not least in its vulgar conceptions of the Divine nature and its glory. The majestic attributes which separate God from man, and make Him unlike His creatures, are the ones which people too often fancy belong to the glorious side of His character. They draw distinctions between "grace" and "glory," and think that the latter applies mainly to what I might call the physical and the metaphysical, and less to the moral attributes of the Divine nature. We adore power, and when it is expanded to infinity we think that it is the glory of God. But my text delivers us from all such misconceptions. If we rightly understand it, then we learn this, that the true heart of the glory is tenderness and love. Of power that weak Man hanging on the cross is a strange embodiment; but if we learn that there is something more godlike in God than power, then we can say, as we look upon Jesus Christ: "Lo! this is our God. We have waited for Him, and He will save us." Not in the wisdom that knows no growth, not in the knowledge which has no border-land of ignorance ringing it round about, not in the unwearied might of His arm, not in the exhaustless energy of His being, not in the unslumbering watchfulness of His all-seeing eye, not in that awful Presence wheresoever creatures are, not in any or in all of these lies the glory of God, but in His love. These are the fringes of the brightness; this is the central blaze. The Gospel is the Gospel of the glory of God, because it is all summed up in the one word—"God so loved the world that He gave His only begotten Son."

Now, in the next place, the revelation of God in Christ is the blessedness of God.

We are come here into places where we see but very dimly, and it becomes us to speak very cautiously. Only as we are led by the Divine teaching may we affirm at all. But it cannot be unwise to accept in simple literality utterances of Scripture, however they may seem to strike us as strange. And so I would say—the philosopher's God may be all-sufficient and unemotional, the Bible's God "delighteth in mercy," rejoiceth in His gifts, and is glad when men accept them. It is something, surely, amid all the griefs and sorrows of this sorrow-haunted and devil-hunted world, to rise to this lofty region and to feel that there is a living personal Joy at the heart of the universe. If we went no further, to me there is infinite beauty and mighty consolation and strength in that one thought—the happy God. He is not, as some ways of representing Him figure Him to be, what the older astronomers thought the sun was, a great cold orb, black and frigid at the heart, though the source and center of light and warmth of the system. But He Himself is Joy, or if we dare not venture on that word, which brings with it earthly associations, and suggests the possibility of alteration—He is the blessed God. And the Psalmist saw deeply into the Divine nature, who, not contented with hymning His praise as the Possessor of the fountain of life, and the Light whereby we see light, exclaimed in an ecstasy of anticipation, "Thou makest us to drink of the rivers of Thy pleasures."

But there is a great deal more than that here, if not in the word itself, at least in its connection, which connection seems to suggest that howsoever the Divine nature must be supposed to be blessed in its own absolute and boundless perfectness, an element in the blessedness of God Himself arises from His self-communication through the Gospel to the world. All love delights in imparting. Why should not God's? On the lower level of human affection we know that it is so, and on the highest level we may with all reverence venture to say, The quality of that mercy. . . . "is twice blest," and that Divine love "blesseth Him that gives and them that take."

He created a universe because He delights in His works and in having creatures on whom He can lavish Himself. He "rests in His love, and rejoices over us with singing" when we open our hearts to the reception of His light, and learn to know Him as He has declared Himself in His Christ. The blessed God is blessed because He is God. But He is blessed too because He is the loving and therefore the giving God.

What a rock-firmness such a thought as this gives to the mercy and the love that He pours out upon us! If they were evoked by our worthiness we might well tremble, but when we know, according to the grand words familiar to many of us, that it is His nature and property to be merciful, and that He is far gladder in giving than we can be in receiving, then we may be sure that His mercy endureth for ever, and that it is the very necessity of His being—and He cannot turn His back upon Himself—to love, to pity, to succor, and to bless.

And so, lastly, the revelation of God in Christ is good news for us all.

"The Gospel of the glory of the blessed God." How that word "gospel" has got tarnished and enfeebled by constant use and unreflective use, so that it slips glibly off my tongue and falls without producing any effect upon your hearts. It needs to be freshened up by considering what really it means. It means this: here are we like men shut up in a beleaguered city, hopeless, helpless, with no power to break out or to raise the siege; provisions failing, death certain. And here to us, prisoned, comes, as it did to them, a despatch borne under a Dove's wing, and the message is this:—God is love; and that you may know that He is, He has sent you His Son Who died on the Cross, the sacrifice for a world's sin. Believe it and trust it, and all your transgressions will pass away.

Is not that good news? Is not *the* good news that you need—the news of a Father, of pardon, of hope, of love, of strength, of purity, of Heaven? Does it not meet our fears, our forebodings, our wants at every point? It comes to you. What do you do with it? Do you welcome it eagerly, do you clutch it to your hearts, do you say, "This is *my* Gospel"? Oh! let me beseech you, welcome the message; do not turn away from the Word from Heaven, which will bring life and blessedness to all your hearts!

VICTORY IN FAILURE

Some of you have turned away long enough, some of you, perhaps, are fighting with the temptation to do so again even now. Let me press that ancient Gospel upon your acceptance, that Christ the Son of God has died for you, and lives to bless and help you. Take it and live! So shall you find that "as cold water to a thirsty soul, so is this best of all news from the far country."